BAN ASSAULT BANANAS

Ban Assault Bananas

Copyright © 2018 by Ken Pealock

All rights reserved. No part of this book may be sed or reproduced in any manner whatsoever without written permission of the author, except in the case of brief quotations embodies in critical articles and review.

Nothing herein should be construed as legal advice. If legal advice is needed, a competent attorney should be sought.

ISBN-13: 978-1718854505

BAN ASSAULT BANANAS

Table of Contents

Introduction 5

Part I

Idiot's Argument #1 11
Idiot's Argument #2 12
Idiot's Argument #3 14
Idiot's Argument #4 17
Idiot's Argument #5 19
Idiot's Argument #6 22
Idiot's Argument #7 27
Idiot's Argument #8 30
Idiot's Argument #9 31
Idiot's Argument #10 36

Part II

The Right to Life 45

Part III

The Right to Resist Tyranny 51

Part IV

Will Tyranny Happen Here? 59

Part V

The Interstate Commerce Scam 69

Appendix

Speeches of Patrick Henry 75
District of Columbia v. Heller 103
United States v. Lopez 170

Three things cannot be long hidden: the sun, the moon, and the truth.
— *Buddha*

Introduction

The outright lies spewed by gun control proponents prompted me to write this book.
Herein, I set the record straight on the major arguments put forth by the uninformed, the idiots and those who easily manipulate them.

I chose the tongue-in-cheek title *Ban Assault Bananas* to express the absurdity of gun control. After all, shoving a banana down someone's throat could kill them, so do we ban every fruit or implement that could be used as a weapon?

A satirical article on cellar.org pointed out the different ways a person could be killed by a banana:

- Slip on a banana peel and crack your head.
- Choke while attempting to eat too much banana.
- Crushed to death under a huge pile of bananas.
- Stabbed to death with a frozen, sharpened banana.
- Hanged or garroted with a rope made from the fibers from a banana peel.
- Choke while attempting to fellate a banana.

I'm not minimizing the tragic death of anyone by firearms or other means, but I must expose the idiotic arguments of those who believe banning guns saves lives. The question is whether an armed or unarmed citizenry saves lives. Herein, I shall prove that *having* guns saves lives. The police use guns to save lives (most of the time), but the police can't be everywhere.

Aside from personal self-defense, private ownership of firearms is our last means of defense against government oppression. We no longer face a threat of foreign invasion: the real threat to liberty comes from within.

Another point to make relative to the idiocy of gun control laws is they don't work to reduce crime. Yes, you will find some statistics that claim crime has been reduced after local gun laws have been passed, and others that say it hasn't changed at all. But what these statistics don't show is the greater number of criminal acts that are prevented simply by displaying a firearm. The majority of these go unreported.

Going a step further, we now see the introduction of plans for 3-D printed guns, partially completed receivers one can purchase online, and blueprints to make one's own firearm. These products are a response to the conspiracy to ban guns.

What the gun control zealots don't realize is that for every action there is an equal or greater reaction. By banning guns, or certain ones, it spurs the development of other means of self-defense. Recently I was privy to seeing a demonstration of an electronic weapon powerful enough to repel an army brigade or squadron of jets. The government has it, and now a small group of patriots have it.

It is a terrible thing for anyone to die, violently or otherwise, but gun bans encourage bad people to kill by more lethal means—bombs and cars, for example. Elon Musk now sells a $500 flamethrower that anyone

BAN ASSAULT BANANAS

can buy without restriction. Imagine the harm caused by a deranged person going into a school or theater with a flamethrower. The carnage would be far worse than with a firearm.

"False is the idea of utility that sacrifices a thousand real advantages for one imaginary or trifling inconvenience; that would take fire from men because it burns, and water because one may drown in it; that has no remedy for evils, except destruction. The laws that forbid the carrying of arms are laws of such a nature. They disarm only those who are neither inclined nor determined to commit crimes.

Can it be supposed that those who have the courage to violate the most sacred laws of humanity, the most important of the code, will respect the less important and arbitrary ones, which can be violated with ease and impunity, and which if strictly obeyed, would put an end to personal liberty -- so dear to men, so dear to the enlightened legislator -- and subject innocent persons to all the vexations that the guilty alone ought to suffer? Such laws make things worse for the assaulted and better for the assailants; they serve rather to encourage than to prevent homicides, for an unarmed man may be attacked with greater confidence than an armed man. They ought to be designated as laws not preventive but fearful of crimes, produced by the tumultuous impression of a few isolated facts, and not by thoughtful consideration of the inconveniences and advantages of a universal decree."

- CESARE BECCARIA, *father of modern criminology, 1764.*

BAN ASSAULT BANANAS

"Gun safety laws, there are a few inconvenient facts... Liberals are sometimes glib about equating guns and danger. In fact, it's complicated. The number of guns in America has increased by more than 50 percent since 1993, and in that same period the gun homicide rate in the United States has dropped by half... The assault weapons ban: A 113-page study found no clear indication that it reduced shooting deaths for the 10 years it was in effect. Move on to open-carry and conceal-carry laws. With some 13 million Americans now licensed to pack a concealed gun, many liberals expected gun battles to be erupting all around us. In fact, the most rigorous analysis suggests that all these gun permits caused neither a drop in crime, as conservatives had predicted, nor a spike in killings, as liberals had expected... The fears were overblown... Liberals often inadvertently antagonize gun owners and empower the National Rifle Association by coming across as supercilious, condescending and spectacularly uninformed about the guns they propose to regulate. A classic of gun ignorance, new York passed a law three years ago banning gun magazines holding more than seven cartridges; without realizing that for most guns there is no such thing as a magazine for seven cartridges or less...!

- NICK KRISTOF, "Some Inconvenient Gun Facts For Liberals", *The New York Times* (January 16, 2016).

Part I

"Government being instituted for the common benefit, protection, and security of the whole community, and not for the private interest or emolument of any one man, family or class of men; therefore, whenever the ends of government are perverted, and pay public liberty manifestly endangered, and all other means of redress are ineffectual, the people may, and of right ought, to reform the old, or establish a new government. The doctrine of non-resistance against arbitrary power, and oppression, is absurd, slavish, and destructive of the good and happiness of mankind."

- New Hampshire Constitution of 1784

BAN ASSAULT BANANAS

Idiot's Argument #1:

The Second Amendment only protects muskets.

Fact:

The Supreme Court in *District of Columbia v. Heller*, 171 L. Ed. 2d 637 (2008) stated:

> Some have made the argument, bordering on the frivolous, that only those arms in existence in the 18th century are protected by the Second Amendment. We do not interpret constitutional rights that way. Just as the First Amendment protects modern forms of communications, e.g., Reno v. American Civil Liberties Union, 521 U. S. 844, 849 (1997), and the Fourth Amendment applies to modern forms of search, e.g., Kyllo v. United States, 533 U. S. 27, 35-36 (2001), **the Second Amendment extends, prima facie, to all instruments that constitute bearable arms, even those that were not in existence at the time of the founding.**

Idiot's Argument #1 is the ludicrous proposition that the militia is restricted to using muskets against an enemy force that has fully-automatic AK-47 rifles!

Idiot's Argument #2:

There must be limits on guns like on free speech: after all, you can't yell "Fire" in a crowded theater.

Fact:

This argument is inapplicable to limits on firearm ownership. Here's where the catchphrase originated:

> *"'Shouting fire in a crowded theater'"* is a popular metaphor for speech or actions made for the principal purpose of creating unnecessary panic. The phrase is a paraphrasing of Oliver Wendell Holmes, Jr.'s opinion in the United States Supreme Court case *Schenck v. United States* in 1919, which held that the defendant's speech in opposition to the draft during World War I was not protected free speech under the First Amendment of the United States Constitution.
>
> The paraphrasing does not generally include (but does usually imply) the word falsely, i.e., "***falsely*** shouting fire in a crowded theater", which was the original wording used in Holmes's opinion and highlights that speech that is dangerous and false is not protected, as opposed to speech that is dangerous but also true.
>
> The First Amendment holding in Schenck was later partially overturned by *Brandenburg v. Ohio* in 1969, which limited the scope of banned speech

to that which would be directed to and likely to incite *imminent lawless action* (e.g. a riot).

The test in Brandenburg is the current Supreme Court jurisprudence on the ability of government to proscribe speech after that fact. Despite Schenck being subsequently limited, the phrase "shouting fire in a crowded theater" has since come to be known as synonymous with an action that the speaker believes goes beyond the rights guaranteed by free speech, reckless or malicious speech, or an action whose outcomes are obvious." *Wikipedia.*

———

The argument is based on the false premise that government has "authority" to restrict firearm ownership. They don't, as we shall see later. But even if they did, this analogy is inapplicable to firearms since mere possession is not likely to incite "imminent lawless action" under the speech test in Brandenburg.

Idiot's Argument #3:

We must have "common-sense" gun control laws.

Fact:

The phrase "common-sense" is yet another open-ended phrase without real meaning. Obama uttered it many times, and others still echo it.

I would like for someone to explain how a politician who swore an oath to uphold the Constitution can call for infringing on the absolute right to possess firearms.

The Second Amendment is quite clear:

> A well regulated Militia, being necessary to the security of a free State, the right of the people to keep and bear Arms, **shall not be infringed.**

In *United States v. Cruikshank* (1876), the Supreme Court ruled that the federal government had no authority to infringe on the right to keep and bear arms:

> "The Second Amendments means no more than that it shall not be **infringed** by Congress, and has no other effect than to restrict the powers of the National Government."

BAN ASSAULT BANANAS

The words, shall not be infringed means **shall not be infringed.** Period. there is no qualifying phrase that says "except for common-sense restrictions." The right to keep and bear arms is absolute and without limitation; this is shown by the word infringe: *fringe* refers to the *outermost fringes* of a garment or agreement:

> *infringe* (in'fringe) vt. [Latinz infringere, to break off, violate, modify or impair] 1. To encroach, restrict, or trespass on even the most peripheral and extreme margins, border or outer edge of a law or agreement, though minor or insignificant in relation to the main part.

The word *infringed* appears only once in the U.S. Constitution and only within the Second Amendment. The fact that it does not appear in any of the other delineations of our rights underscores the significance and primacy which the Framers placed on the right to keep and bear arms. It was only by armed resistance of individuals that British tyranny was ended; years of pleadings and petitions had failed.

The Framers learned the hard way that tyrants don't willingly give up power, and that tyranny wasn't limited to the Crown. Therefore, the newly *Free and Independent States* demanded that the proposed Constitution incorporate a guarantee that individuals would always have the means to resist federal government tyranny if it ever became necessary.

Conclusive proof of this is contained in the historical records of the Ratification Debates. These debates eventually led to adoption of the first 10 Amendments known as the Bill of Rights. Perhaps

BAN ASSAULT BANANAS

the most enlightening speeches during these constitutional debates were those made by super-patriot Patrick Henry at the Virginia Ratifying Convention on June 5 and 7, 1788.

> Guard with jealous attention the public liberty. Suspect every one who approaches that jewel. Unfortunately, nothing will preserve it, but downright force. Whenever you give up that force, you are inevitably ruined...I conceive of this new Government to be one of those dangers...I will submit to your recollection, whether liberty has been destroyed most often by the licentiousness of the people or by the tyranny of rulers? I imagine, Sir, you will find the balance on the side of tyranny...
>
> My great objection to this Government is, that it does not leave us the means of defending our rights or, of waging war against tyrants [in the federal government]...Have we the means of resisting disciplined armies, when our only defence (sic), the militia is put into the hands of Congress?

It is indisputable, therefore, that the people must have, and do have, an *unlimited* right to the same weapons the government can use against them. How can the people protect themselves from the government when their means of protection from it are determined by the federal government itself? A fox guarding the henhouse?

Although subsequent Supreme Court rulings *claim* there are "limits" to the types of firearms individuals can own, these judicial opinions violate the 2nd Amendment and their oath of office.

Idiot's Argument #4:

The Second Amendment applies to the militia—not individuals.

Fact:

The Supreme Court ruled in *District of Columbia v. Heller* that the Second Amendment protects the right of individuals to keep and bear arms. The argument that it applied to only the militia is nonsensical and belies the historical record. The Heller decision stated:

> The Second Amendment is naturally divided into two parts: its prefatory clause and its operative clause. The former does not limit the latter grammatically, but rather announces a purpose. The Amendment could be rephrased, "Because a well regulated Militia is necessary to the security of a free State, the right of the people to keep and bear Arms shall not be infringed."
> Logic demands that there be a link between the stated purpose and the command. But apart from that clarifying function, a prefatory clause does not limit or expand the scope of the operative clause.
> Operative Clause: "Right of the People." The first salient feature of the operative clause is that it codifies a "right of the people." The unamended Constitution and the Bill of Rights use the phrase "right of the people" two other times, in the First Amendment's Assembly-and-Petition Clause and

in the Fourth Amendment's Search-and-Seizure Clause. The Ninth Amendment uses very similar terminology ("The enumeration in the Constitution, of certain rights, shall not be construed to deny or disparage others retained by the people"). All three of these instances unambiguously refer to individual rights, not "collective" rights, or rights that may be exercised only through participation in some corporate body.

Nowhere else in the Constitution does a "right" attributed to "the people" refer to anything other than an individual right. What is more, in all six other provisions of the Constitution that mention "the people," the term unambiguously refers to all members of the political community, not an unspecified subset.

This contrasts markedly with the phrase "the militia" in the prefatory clause. As we will describe below, the "militia" in colonial America consisted of a subset of "the people"– those who were male, able bodied, and within a certain age range. Reading the Second Amendment as protecting only the right to "keep and bear Arms" in an organized militia therefore fits poorly with the operative clause's description of the holder of that right as "the people."

We move now from the holder of the right – "the people" – to the substance of the right: "to keep and bear Arms." From our review of founding-era sources, we conclude that this natural meaning was also the meaning that "bear arms" had in the 18th century. In numerous instances, "bear arms" was unambiguously used to refer to the carrying of weapons outside of an organized militia. It is clear from those formulations that "bear arms" did not refer only to carrying a weapon in an organized military unit.

BAN ASSAULT BANANAS

Idiot's Argument #5:

AR-15-style assault rifles should be restricted to the military.

Fact:

First, the military definition of an "assault rifle" means a *fully-automatic* rifle used by the military—not the semi-auto AR-15 and others sold to civilians. The "assault" label serves to inflame the public into supporting legislation to outlaw them. Yet, again, the purported guarantees of the Second Amendment provide that civilians "keep and bear"the same arms the enemy possesses. That includes their use, as a last resort, against a tyrannical federal government that seeks to disarm them.

The Second Amendment says the federal government has no lawful authority to infringe—i.e., to regulate, ban or criminalize the possession of *any* type of firearm. This includes so-called assault rifles, pistols, machineguns, silencers, bump stocks, or ammunition. It means that every person whose firearm has been seized or who has been imprisoned on federal firearm charges or had them seized by federal agents is the *victim* of a crime—not the perpetrator. The Constitution is the law of the land, and for laws to be valid they cannot be contrary to the Constitution:

U.S. Constitution, Article VI

This Constitution, and the laws of the United States which shall be made in pursuance thereof; and all treaties made, or which shall be made, under the authority of the United States, **shall be the supreme law of the land;** and the judges in every state shall be bound thereby, anything in the Constitution or laws of any State to the contrary notwithstanding.

The President, Congress, judges and federal law enforcement agents take an oath to support the Constitution—not to support case precedent, treaties, or other laws in opposition to the *supreme law of the land* and the Bill of Rights.

Further, every official, including congressmen, judges, and federal agents, who conspires, advocates, enforces, or by any other means upholds unconstitutional federal laws is engaged in a criminal conspiracy under color of law:

UNITED STATES CODE
TITLE 18 - CRIMES AND CRIMINAL PROCEDURE
PART I - CRIMES CHAPTER 13 - CIVIL RIGHTS
§ 241. Conspiracy against rights

If two or more persons conspire to injure, oppress, threaten, or intimidate any inhabitant of any State, Territory, or District in the free exercise or enjoyment of any right or privilege secured to him by the Constitution or laws of the United States, or because of his having so exercised the same; or

If two or more persons go in disguise on the highway, or on the premises of another, with intent to prevent or hinder his free exercise or enjoyment of any right or privilege so secured -

BAN ASSAULT BANANAS

They shall be fined not more than $10,000 or imprisoned not more than ten years, or both; and if death results, they shall be subject to imprisonment for any term of years or for life.

We now live, to put it mildly, under a system that operates completely outside the limits provided by the Constitution.

Idiot's Argument #6:
The National Guard will protect us from a tyrannical federal government.

Fact:

The so-called National Guard is *not* a state militia and it is not the militia of the whole people. The Supreme Court admitted as much in *Perpich v. Department of Defense,* 496 US 334 (1990). Governor Perpich and the State of Minnesota challenged the constitutionality of a statue that prevented the governor from withholding his consent to a training mission in Central America in 1987.

The Supreme Court disagreed with Governor Perpich:

> Since 1933 all persons who have enlisted in a State National Guard unit have simultaneously enlisted in the National Guard of the United States. In the latter capacity they became a part of the Enlisted Reserve Corps of the Army, but unless and until ordered to active duty in the Army, they retained their status as members of a separate State Guard unit.... In a sense, all of them now must keep three hats in their closets—a civilian hat, a state militia hat, and an army hat—only one of which is worn at any particular time.

BAN ASSAULT BANANAS

[However] Congress has provided by statute that in addition to its National Guard, a State may provide and maintain at its own expense a defense force that is exempt from being drafted into the Armed Forces of the United States.

Thus, the "National Guard of the United States" is *not* a militia organized to protect the inhabitants of a state from federal tyranny. In fact, its primary function is to "suppress insurrections" *against* the federal government. See U.S. Constitution, Article I- clauses 15 and 16 of §8.

The referenced state-financed militias, such as the Georgia Defense Force, are not a realistic protection from the federal government and its vast resources of men and materiel. Even worse, despite the statutory exemptions from state-financed militia being drafted into the Armed Forces of the United States, the Perpich court stated in footnote 25 that members "might" still be drafted into the military under statue 10 USCS §§331-333.

Thus, the only protection we have from an oppressive federal government is a heavily armed citizenry—i.e., a *private* militia composed of the body of the people—like those excoriated by the press.

Though the militia clauses in the Constitution were seen as a bulwark against federal tyranny, not everyone was fooled. A few recognized the protection was more illusory than real. One such person was Patrick Henry, who spoke during the Virginia Ratifying Convention on June 5 and 7, 1788:

> My great objection to this Government is, that it does not leave us the means of defending our rights or, of waging war against tyrants [in the

federal government]...Have we the means of resisting disciplined armies, when our only defence (sic), the militia is put into the hands of Congress.

A standing army we shall have also, to execute the execrable commands of tyranny: And how are you to punish them? Will you order them to be punished? Who shall obey these orders?...Your militia is given to Congress...They will therefore act as they think proper: All power will be in their possession: You cannot force them to receive their punishment: Of what service would militia be to you, when most probably you will not have a single musket in the State; for as arms are to be provided by Congress, they may or may not furnish them.

Let me call your attention to that part which gives Congress power, "To providing for organizing, arming, and disciplining the militia, and for governing such part of them as may be employed in the service of the United States, reserving to the States respectively, the appointment of the officers, and the authority of training the Militia, according to the discipline prescribed by Congress." By this, Sir, you see that their control over our last and best defence (sic), is unlimited. If they neglect or refuse to discipline or arm our militia, they will be useless: The States can do neither, this power being exclusively given to Congress:

The power of appointing officers over men not disciplined or armed, is ridiculous: So that this pretended little remains of power left to the States, may, at the pleasure of Congress, be rendered nugatory.

Will the oppressor let go of the oppressed? Was there ever an instance? Can the annals of mankind exhibit one single example where rulers overcharged with power, willingly let go of the oppressed, though solicited and requested most earnestly?...A willing relinquishment of power is one of those things which human nature never was, nor ever will be capable of...Will the great rights of the people be secured by this Government? Suppose it should prove oppressive, how can it be altered?

Since all military power is now in the hands of the federal government, what will happen when all private citizens are eventually disarmed and helpless to resist? We know that we can't rely on the Constitution to prevent tyranny—the courts routinely ignore that musty piece of parchment. Here's what a former Justice of the Supreme Court had to say:

> "The Constitution as many of us understood it, the Constitution that has meant so much to us, is gone. The guarantees that men and women have supposed protected them against arbitrary action have been swept away."
> — Justice McReynolds, *dissenting in a 1935 decision removing gold backing for the Dollar.*

More recently, the late Supreme Court Justice Antonin Scalia lamented that "Day by day, case by case, the Supreme Court is writing a new Constitution I no longer recognize."

Over the years many other Justices have likewise complained that the Supreme Court has interpreted away the entire Bill of Rights. It doesn't take an Einstein to understand why Oliver Wendell Holmes called the Supreme Court "Nine scorpions in a bottle" more than 50 years ago.

BAN ASSAULT BANANAS

When even Justices of the highest Court in the land are admitting that we have no real constitutional protections left, something is seriously wrong—tyranny not only *can* happen, it *has* happened.

Idiot's Argument #7:

The Brady Bill prevents criminals from possessing firearms.

Fact:

The Brady Bill is a fraudulent and unconstitutional act of Congress. First, let's review what the Brady Bill (Act) has allegedly accomplished. According to FBI reports, 100 million Brady Act background checks resulted in 700,000 denials of firearm purchases. These denials are based on data submitted into the FBI's National Instant Criminal Background Check System (NCIS) by the FBI, ATF, state, local, other federal law enforcement agencies, and physicians.

Those disqualified included people:

- who've been convicted of a felony.
- under indictment for a felony.
- adjudged mentally ill.
- dishonorably discharged from the military.
- who've renounced their American citizenship.
- considered "illegal aliens" and legal aliens under a non-immigrant visa.
- under a restraining order for domestic violence or convicted for it.
- with a history of drug abuse.
- with multiple DUIs.
- The list keeps growing.

BAN ASSAULT BANANAS

Fact #1: The above figure of 700,000 people denied a firearm by the FBI is misleading. It doesn't mean they don't possess a firearm. Most who were denied *already own one or more firearms!*

Fact #2: These figures do not prove that 700,000 people would have "committed a crime" using those firearms. However, it does prove that *the FBI committed a crime against 700,000 people.*

Fact #3: The Brady Bill is 100% unconstitutional because, under the due process clause, you cannot deny someone a right based on what they *might* do with a firearm. When "mights and maybes" are the basis of laws, then we live in a police state and everyone is a criminal.

Fact #4: The Brady Bill pretends to restrict the FBI from compiling or retaining a database of the names of gun owners. Years ago, however, and unnoticed by many, a lawsuit was filed against the Bureau of Alcohol, Firearms and Tobacco (BATF, now BATFE) for retaining purchaser records for six months (but probably much longer). The court dismissed the lawsuit, blatantly ignoring the law itself. The court said six months was "reasonable."

Other proof: (1) whenever a dealer goes out of business his 4473 Firearm Transaction Records go straight into ATF and FBI records. (2) whenever a physician submits mandatory information on a patient who has seizures or mental issues, that record goes into government files. *(3)* the NSA, and Homeland Security spy on every American. They collect records of phone calls, faces, internet searches, and everything that is known about you—including your subscriptions to gun magazines and gun-related purchases. The IRS also has access to purchase records through your bank and credit card records.

Fact #5: Several states have enacted their own background checks, which include sales made over the internet and at gun shows. That information is freely given to the FBI.

Fact #6: The creation of a registry of firearms owners is, historically, the first step toward confiscation. It is an infringement of the Second Amendment and the right to privacy.

Idiot's Argument #8:

Felons should be barred from owning firearms.

Fact:

Once again, the Second Amendment says **"shall not be infringed."** It does *not* say, "except for felons and others that the government decides shouldn't have firearms." Should the Founders have been banned from owning a firearm? After all, they committed felonious treason against the Crown.

Whenever government has the power to decide who can own a firearm, then that right becomes a privilege that becomes more restricted over time. For example, the prohibition against convicted or indicted felons owning a firearm can be expanded to *unindicted* felons. According to attorney Harvey Silvergate, the average person commits three felonies a day without realizing it. His book, *Three Felonies A Day*, is an indictment of the thousands of laws and regulations that result in almost everyone committing a felony.

Ask yourself these questions:

- Have you ever "cheated" even one penny on your taxes?

BAN ASSAULT BANANAS

- Have you ever given someone a single prescription pill or liquid that was prescribed for you?
- Have you ever photocopied or downloaded any copyrighted publications or music without permission?
- Have you ever failed to *report* a felony committed by a family member, neighbor, or friend?
- Have you ever made false statements to any government official?
- Have you ever violated an EPA restriction you didn't know about?
- Have you ever killed an animal that you didn't know was endangered?
- Have you and another person ever *thought* about committing any of the above?

If you've done any of these thing, or violated some 20,000 federal regulations carrying criminal penalties that you don't even know about, then you are a felon—unconvicted perhaps, but a felon nonetheless.

Idiot's Argument #9:

The mentally ill should be barred from owning firearms.

Fact:

The late Supreme Court Justice Antonin Scalia said that the most important question in jurisprudence is "Who decides?"

At present, anyone with PTSD is disqualified from owning a firearm. Large numbers of military men fighting in the Middle East return home with post–traumatic stress disorder or clinical depression. In fact, the majority of Americans suffer from depression at some point.

So who decides whether a person is disqualified from owning a firearm based on mental illness? Congress or some bureaucrat writing regulations? And who is to stop him from acquiring one from an individual under the alleged "gun show loophole" in the Brady Act?

Rather than passing idiotic "feel-good" laws that criminals disobey, let's solve the problem with facts. Thomas Sowell asks the relevant question: *"Who is more mentally unbalanced, those who are doing the shooting or those who refuse to examine the facts about what kinds of places attract such shooters?"*

BAN ASSAULT BANANAS

"Almost invariably, mass shootings occur in gun-free settings. Yet gun control zealots seem determined to create more gun-free settings. How often have supposedly mentally unbalanced shooters opened fire at a meeting of the National Rifle Association? They are apparently not that mentally unbalanced. They pick places where people are not likely to shoot back. A mass shooting at a movie theater a few years ago took place at a theater farther away from where the shooter lived than other theaters in the area that were showing the very same movie. The difference was that this theater had advertised that it was a gun-free zone. Who is more mentally unbalanced, those who are doing the shooting or those who refuse to examine the facts about what kinds of places attract such shooters? Schools and religious institutions are sitting ducks, and the shootings there have gone on until someone else with a gun showed up on the scene. That is what puts an end to the carnage, not gun control laws. People who are prepared to defy the laws against murder are not very likely to be stopped by laws against guns. Only law-abiding citizens are likely to be stopped by gun control laws, and to become sitting ducks.

As for facts and statistics, the only ones likely to be mentioned by gun control zealots, including the media, are those on how many people were killed by guns. How many lives were saved by guns will never make it through the ideological filters of the media, the political establishment or our educational institutions. Yet factual data on how many threats or attacks were deterred in a given year by displaying a firearm have long been available. Seldom is it necessary to actually pull the trigger to get some thug or criminal to back off and go elsewhere, often in some haste. Are the

only lives that matter those that are lost, usually because there is no gun immediately available to protect them, but not the lives saved because they did have a gun at hand to protect them? Gun control zealots seem especially opposed to people being allowed to carry their guns concealed. But concealed weapons protect not only those who carry them, but also to some extent those who do not, because criminals have no way of knowing in advance who does and does not have a gun. Muggings and rapes become much more dangerous activities for criminals where many law-abiding people are allowed to carry concealed guns. It can take a lot of the fun out of being a thug.
 -Thomas Sowell, "Showman-in-Chief", *Jewish World Review* (January 6, 2016)

Carl Sagan once wrote that if an alien species were to observe the human race, they would conclude that *everyone* was crazy. But, of course, there is a difference between being "crazy" and the wide range of what is defined as mentally ill. What we see is a means of confiscation by criminalizing the possession of firearms.

But since "mass shootings" seems to be the current focus of gun control zealots, let's take a look at the statistics. First, the definition of a mass shooting varies. Michael Bloomberg's gun violence prevention group, *Everytown for Gun Safety*, identified 110 mass shooting, defined as shootings in which at least four people were murdered with a firearm, between January 2009 and July 2014. Admitted was that 57% were related to domestic or family violence—not the indiscriminate rampages in

BAN ASSAULT BANANAS

public places that we commonly associate with a mass shooting.

The *Washington Post* reports that in 2018 alone, the police shot and killed 1,000 people. That's more than were killed in mass shootings, and many of those killed by the police were unarmed.

Another statistic is that gun deaths are mostly from suicide. According to an October 8, 2015 *New York Times* article, "More than 60 percent of people in this country who die from guns die from suicide."

And, according to *Science Daily,* the leading cause for injury and death among children is choking, especially among those younger than 4 years of age. In fact, choking was the fourth most common cause of unintentional injury-related death in the US in 2011. According to the National Safety Council, deaths from choking most often occur in the very young (children under 1 years old) and in the elderly (adults over 75 years).

By the way, Mama Cass Elliot, known as "Mama Cass", of the group The Mamas and the Papas did *not* die from choking on a ham sandwich. The cause of death was "heart failure due to fatty myocardial degeneration due to obesity."

Speaking of obesity, we have over 300,000 deaths per year from obesity. That's 25,000 per month, 5,769 per week, 821 per day, 34 per hour. This calculation comes from the annual 300,000 premature deaths the CDC associates with obesity.

By comparison, FBI statistics show 11,961 *annual* deaths from firearm homicides. So where is the outrage and mass protests for "common-sense" food controls? Look at the lives we'd save with strict limits on who can eat dangerous "assault hamburgers" and french fries. We should ban bananas too.

BAN ASSAULT BANANAS

We must recognize that death comes to everyone sooner or later. According to the CDC, the leading causes of death for the U.S. are:

- Heart disease: 635,260
- Cancer: 598,038
- Accidents: 161,374
- Chronic lower respiratory diseases: 154,596
- Stroke (cerebrovascular diseases): 142,142
- Alzheimer's disease: 116,103
- Diabetes: 80,058
- Influenza and pneumonia: 51,537
- Nephritis, nephrotic syndrome, and nephrosis: 50,046
- Intentional self-harm (suicide): 44,965

Source: Health United States, 2017 Table 19 (Data are for 2016)

Missing from these statistics are the 106,000 annual death from prescription drugs (out of 783,936 annual deaths from conventional medical mistakes).

You may be interested to know that the overall number of annual U.S. deaths is 2,712,630, or a death rate of 844 per 100,000 population. Gun homicides, by my research, shows only 4.5 deaths per 100,000 population.

We can't stop death itself, at least not yet, but what we can do is stop falling prey to the misguided gun zealots. If people don't want their children being killed in public schools, then take them out of government schools and teach them at home and away from the drugs and government propaganda.

BAN ASSAULT BANANAS

Idiot's Argument #10:
There is no conspiracy to ban private ownership of firearms.

Fact:

Every official, including congressmen, judges, and federal agents, who advocates, enforces, or upholds *unconstitutional* federal laws on firearm possession is engaged in a criminal conspiracy under color of law. See Title 18 U.S.C. § 241. Here's the admissions of a few conspirators:

- "If I could have gotten 51 votes in the Senate of the United States for an outright ban, picking up every one of them, Mr. and Mrs. America, turn them all in, I would have done it."
—*Sen. Dianne Feinstein, CBS 60 Minutes, 2/5/95*

- "Banning guns is an idea whose time has come."
—*U.S. Sen. Joseph Biden, Associated Press, 11/18/93*

- "They should demand a repeal of the Second Amendment."
—*Former U.S. Supreme Court Justice John Paul Stevens*

BAN ASSAULT BANANAS

- "There is no reason for anyone in the country, for anyone except a police officer or a military person, to own, to have, to use, a handgun. The only way to control handgun use in this country is to prohibit the guns. And the only way to do that is to change the Constitution."
  —*NBC President Michael Gartner, USA TODAY, 1992*

- "Let's take all the handguns we have in America, put them on a couple of old rusted ships, take them out in the middle of the ocean and sink them, that would be the best thing to do."
  —*Sen. Tom Harkin, Senate Democratic Policy Committee Hearing, 5/15/2000*

- Assault weapons play a part in only a small percentage of crime. [The ban's] virtue will be if it turns out to be, as hoped, a stepping stone to broader gun control."
  —*The Washington Post, editorial, 9/15/94*

- "No, we are not looking at how to control criminals, we are talking about banning...guns!"
  —*Sen. Howard Metzenbaum, Constitution Subcommittee Hearings, 2/10/89*

- "If it were up to me we'd ban all guns."
  —*Rep. Mel Reynolds, CNN Crossfire, 12/9/93*

- "Let's ban them...Let's change the Constitution...There is no reason for anyone in this country, except a police officer or a military person, to buy, to own, to have, to use a handgun."
  —*NBC TV News President Michael Gartner, USA Today, 1/16/92*

BAN ASSAULT BANANAS

- "We're going to beat guns into submission."
  —*Rep. Charles Schumer, news conference, 12/12/93*

- "Banning guns addresses a fundamental right of all Americans to feel safe."
  —*U.S. Senator-elect Dianne Feinstein, Associated Press, 11/18/93*

- "You are not allowed to own a gun and if you do own a gun, I think you should go to prison."
  —*Rosie O'Donnell, The Rosie O'Donnell Show, 4/21/99*

- "The Second Amendment does not extend an individual right to keep and bear arms."
  —*Seth Waxman, position of the Clinton/Gore U.S. Department of Justice, 8/22/2000*

- "The country] can't be so fixated on our desire to preserve the rights of ordinary Americans to legitimately own handguns and rifles."
  —*President Bill Clinton, The Washington Post, 3/2/93*

Incremental Gun Confiscation

These admissions prove there is on-going conspiracy to ban the private ownership of firearms. Justice Stevens and others call for a "repeal" of the Second Amendment, as it the right to defend one's life depends on the Second Amendment. The fact is that the right to self-preservation is a fundamental right that supersedes all man-made laws.

Since politicians know an outright ban is not political feasible, their strategy continues to be *incremental gun confiscation.*

BAN ASSAULT BANANAS

Banning certain groups is part of it, but there are other means you may not be aware of. *Constructive possession* laws are another scheme whereby disqualified persons can be imprisoned for merely having *access* to a firearm or ammunition. For example, if you are living with another person who has a firearm in their house or car, then you have access to it. The law considers it the same as possession.

What this means is that whomever you live with must get rid of their firearms. Otherwise, the felon (or otherwise disqualified person) will be arrested for constructive possession, and the firearm owner will also be arrested. His charge: "conspiring or aiding and abetting" the possession of a firearm by a disqualified person. This is back-door gun confiscation. With some 20-million Americans with felony convictions effectively disarmed, there must be another 30 to 40 million household members who are likewise disarmed.

I met a man who had multiple misdemeanor traffic violations: driving with expired license, no insurance, and a speeding ticket. In his state, that made him a felon and he was sent to prison. After his release, he entered Walmart with his girlfriend to help her select a pistol for self-defense and pointed to the one in the case that would be suitable for her. He didn't expect the clerk to hand it to *him* for inspection and immediately handed it to his girlfriend. The problem was his parole officer happened to see the event and arrested him for *constructive possession* of a firearm by a convicted felon. Because he had the prior felony, he is now serving a 20-year prison sentence.

BAN ASSAULT BANANAS

Even worse, there is a federal case where a member of a motorcycle club was arrested and imprisoned for constructive possession of a firearm. In this instance, his bodyguard carried a firearm and somehow that made the motorcyclist guilty of constructive possession.

The banning of firearm ownership by disqualified individuals also extends to *ammunition,* which the government defines as "explosive devices." Let me give you an example:

Al Lytle received a 15-year prison sentence for possessing two .22 caliber cartridges. He was moving some furniture out of his deceased father's house when the .22 cartridges fell out. Rather than toss them in the yard where some kid would get hold of them, Al stuck them in his pocket to dispose of properly. On the way home, he was stopped for allegedly speeding and a policeman claimed to recognize the cartridges in his pocket. Because he was a convicted "felon" he was arrested and sent to prison.

One you are on the ever-growing list of disqualified individuals, you and everyone around you are in jeopardy of arrest and imprisonment. I know a man who was *returned* to prison when his parole officer spotted a shotgun shell in his driveway; it had inadvertently fallen out of a truck belonging to friends of his who'd came to visit him.

The chilling effect of imprisonment leads to voluntary gun disposal by those who aren't on the list. One such chilling effect was the infamous raid on the Branch Davidian *church* (not "compound") in

Waco, Texas. This was a publicity raid and a warning to all gun owners. Prior to the raid, Attorney General Janet Reno stated that "America's love affair with guns is coming to an end." This murderous raid needs no further discussion here, except to point out that the FBI and ATF deliberately started the fire that engulfed 86 men, women and children. Here is an excerpt from my other book, *They Left No Crime Uncommitted:*

> The feds were angry because four of their agents were killed in the shootout. However, former FBI agent Ted Gunderson reports that four of the ATF agents were shot from the helicopters, right between the eyes, and they happened to be former bodyguards of Bill Clinton.
> Before this massacre took place, the FBI terrorized them day and night with amplified sounds of dying rabbits. At the time this occurred, I happened to be watching the uncensored satellite feed at my home. Before the fire started, federal agents were already inside the building with a camera. Agents said, "They have some kerosene and hay in the corner – let's get it." I saw the video of the darkened room and heard this statement – once. It was never presented on the news. Clearly, the Davidians did not man a camera and uplink to a satellite, nor refer to themselves as "they."
> The subsequent government disinformation on how the fire started was that military-grade tear gas canisters "accidentally" started the fire. Yet, it was later revealed that the fire department was ordered to stay back and let the building and the people inside burn.

PART II

BAN ASSAULT BANANAS

According to a 1993 study, there were more than 2.2 million defensive gun uses each year in the United States.
— *Gary Kleck and Marc Gertz,* "Results from the National Self-Defense Survey," 1998.

THE RIGHT TO LIFE

privilege (priv-i-lege) n. [Latin privilegum, an exceptional law for or against an individual] 1. A favor, license, permission, advantage, or immunity specially granted to one; esp., a favor given to a certain individual, group, or class, and withheld from certain others, or all others.

Certainly the most fundamental of all rights is the right to life and this right does not come from the Second Amendment nor depend on it. The right to life is meaningless without the ability to protect your life. It is likewise a violation to restrict that right in any manner—whether with waiting periods, licensing fees, or restrictions on your ability to defend yourself. This includes bans on magazine capacity and weapons of any kind that might be necessary to defend yourself against those who would take your life or your freedom.

Unfortunately, government officials and their supporters believe the right to life is a mere *"privilege"* to be licensed, restricted, limited, or denied as they see fit. To put this in perspective, imagine picking up a newspaper and reading the following headline:

ACT OF CONGRESS MAKES RIGHT TO LIFE A PRIVILEGE.
States to issue permits.

Most Americans would be shocked to read such a headline, yet this is exactly what has already happened. It just wasn't published in the mainstream media.

Firearm restrictions, licenses, and various permits seditiously *convert a right into a privilege*. A license grants you "immunity" from prosecution for committing what would otherwise be a crime or other violation of law.

Violent vs. Non-Violent

I mentioned earlier that the government has no lawful or moral right to criminalize possession of firearms by felons and other categories of prohibited persons. In regards to felons, which everyone is, whether convicted or not, most offenders are non-violent. Should a person be denied the right to protect himself and his family because he cheated on his taxes, which almost everyone does? If they are truly violent, then they should stay in prison. But the problem is that the government continues to classify many non-violent crimes as "violent." There is no end to their trickery.

The government wants you to be afraid of gun violence so that you will accept more gun control laws. But this does not mean the government is interested in protecting you from violent crimes.

What you may know is that some of the most violent criminals are those from third-world countries. What you probably don't know, however, is that even those who've committed the most heinous crimes imaginable are not classified as criminals or felons in *this* country. This is because the Supreme Court ruled in 2006 that federal prohibitions against felons purchasing firearms do not apply to crimes committed in other countries—no matter how grisly. See *Small v. United States, 545 U.S. 385* (2005). Does the ban on felons possessing firearms mean anything?

BAN ASSAULT BANANAS

If it still isn't clear to you that the political agenda isn't to protect you, but to disarm you, a real-life example might convince you.

On June 15, 2001 a cab driver named John Lutters was stabbed in the neck by a passenger with a pair of scissors—a deadly weapon not subject to a Brady Bill check. Lutters managed to get a wrist lock on the attacker, Travis Hazelwood. Just as the passenger was about to stab him again, Lutters grabbed his own handgun and killed Hazelwood. Still hemorrhaging from the neck wound, Lutters managed to drive himself to the hospital and survived the ordeal.

The shooting was ruled to be self-defense, but this didn't mean that Lutter's legal problems were over. A prosecutor named Jack Doyle brought felony charges against John Lutter for not having a "permit" to carry a gun in his cab. Under Connecticut law no permit was required to keep a handgun "within the dwelling house or place of business of such person." Lutter's place of business was his cab; and in 2002, Superior Court Judge Lubble Harper, Jr. dismissed the permit charge against Lutters.

But this didn't stop prosecutor Doyle. He appealed to the Connecticut Supreme Court, arguing that a cab is not a "place of business." Doyle won and Lutters lost. Never mind that the law doesn't say that a place of business must be a fixed location: the majority of judges "interpreted" the law that way. Acting unlawfully as legislators, they effectively rewrote the law.

After years of fighting the corrupt court system, Lutters no longer feels safe driving a cab. You see, he's now a "convicted felon" and is barred from possessing a firearm—this time even in his dwelling place. Is Lutters a violent criminal who should be deprived of his right to self-defense?

Governments never admit they intend to limit or completely deny your right to self-preservation; instead, they intend to deprive you of the *means* to protect your life. After all, they have their gated communities and *armed* security teams to protect themselves, all paid for by taxpayers they scheme to disarm.

> "The right of self-defense is the first law of nature: in most governments it has been the study of rulers to confine this right within the narrowest limits possible. Whenever standing armies are kept up, and when the right of the people to keep and bear arms is, under any color or pretext whatsoever, prohibited, liberty, if not already annihilated, is on the brink of destruction."
> - HENRY ST. GEORGE TUCKER, quoted in *Blackstone's 1768 Commentaries on the Laws of England*.

PART III

BAN ASSAULT BANANAS

There is no crueler tyranny than that which is perpetuated under the shield of law and in the name of justice.
—*Charles Montesquieu*

BAN ASSAULT BANANAS

THE RIGHT TO RESIST TYRANNY

So far, we've primarily discussed the right of self-defense against those who would do us harm. Yet another danger we face is the current usurpation of power by the federal government. This was recognized by figures from our past who argued that private ownership of firearms is necessary to defend ourselves against government tyranny.

"Congress has no power to disarm the militia. Their swords and every terrible implement of the soldier are the birthright of Americans. The unlimited power of the sword is not in the hands of either the federal or state governments but where, I trust in God, it will always remain, in the hands of the people."
- TENCH COXE, *The Pennsylvania Gazette* (20 February 1788)

"Before a standing army can rule, the people must be disarmed; as they are in almost every kingdom of Europe. The supreme power in America cannot enforce unjust laws by the sword; because the whole body of the people are armed, and constitute a force superior to any bands of regular troops that can be, on any pretense, raised in the United States."
- NOAH WEBSTER, quoted in *An Examination Into the Leading Principles of the Constitution* (17 October 1787)

"The corollary, from the first position, is, that the right of the people to keep and bear arms shall not be infringed. The prohibition is general. No clause in the Constitution could by any rule of construction be conceived to give to Congress a power to disarm the people. Such a flagitious attempt could only be made under some general pretense by a state legislature.

But if in any blind pursuit of inordinate power, either should attempt it, this amendment may be appealed to as a restraint on both...".

- WILLIAM RAWLE, *A View of the Constitution* (1829)

"And what country can preserve its liberties if their rulers are not warned from time to time that their people preserve the spirit of resistance? Let them take arms. The remedy is to set them right as to facts, pardon and pacify them. What signify a few lives lost in a century or two? The tree of liberty must be refreshed from time to time with the blood of patriots and tyrants. It is its natural manure."

- THOMAS JEFFERSON, in a letter to William Stephens Smith, quoted in Padover's *Jefferson On Democracy*.

"My great objection to this government is that it does not leave us the means of defending our rights or of waging war against tyrants."

- PATRICK HENRY, June 5, 1788.

"The right of the citizens to keep and bear arms has justly been considered, as the palladium of the liberties of a republic; since it offers a strong moral check against the usurpation and arbitrary power of rulers; and will generally, even if these are successful in the first instance, enable the people to resist and triumph over them."

-JOSEPH STORY, U.S. Supreme Court Justice, in his *Commentaries on the Constitution of the United States* (1833), vol. 3, pp. 746-747.

BAN ASSAULT BANANAS

"The rights of conscience, of bearing arms, of changing the government are declared to be inherent in the people."
- FISHER AMES, June 12, 1789.

More recent comments on the right to resist tyranny include:

"The majority falls prey to the delusion, popular in some circles, that ordinary people are too careless and stupid to own guns, and we would be far better off leaving all weapons in the hands of professionals on the government payroll. But the simple truth, born of experience, is that tyranny thrives best where government need not fear the wrath of an armed people... A revolt by Nat Turner and a few dozen other armed blacks could be put down without much difficulty; one by four million armed blacks would have meant big trouble. All too many of the other great tragedies of history, Stalin's atrocities, the killing fields of Cambodia, the Holocaust, to name but a few, were perpetrated by armed troops against unarmed populations. Many could well have been avoided or mitigated, had the perpetrators known their intended victims were equipped with a rifle and twenty bullets apiece, as the Militia Act required here. ...If a few hundred Jewish fighters in the Warsaw Ghetto could hold off the Wehrmacht for almost a month with only a handful of weapons, six million Jews armed with rifles could not so easily have been herded into cattle cars."
- ALEX KOZINSKI, Circuit Judge, dissenting in *Silveira v. Lockyer*, 312 F.3d 1052 (9th Cir. 2002)

"The historical record provides compelling evidence that racism underlies gun control laws; and not in any subtle way. Throughout much of American history, gun control was openly stated as a method for keeping blacks and Hispanics 'in their place', and to quiet the racial fears of whites."
- CLAYTON E. CRAMER, *"The Racist Roots of Gun Control."*

The Militia Scam

The militia is covered in great detail in the landmark *Heller v. District of Columbia* Supreme Court case reprinted in the appendix. We've already mentioned *Perpich v. Department of Defense,* showing that the National Guard is not the militia you may think. In fact, it was designed to protect the federal government *from* the people—not to protect us from a tyrannical federal government.

The nature of the militia was changed even further by Theodore Roosevelt back in 1901, when he declared "Our militia law is obsolete and worthless." His argument, which was the same as that of federalist Alexander Hamilton, was that a civilian militia would not be capable of standing up to a trained military from another nation.

The process of transforming "the National Guard of the several states" then began with the Orwellian-named Dick Act. The Act of January 21, 1903, 32 Stat 775 provided in part:

"That the militia shall consist of every able-bodied male citizen of the respective States, Territories, and the District of Columbia, and every able-bodied male of foreign birth who has declared his intention to become a citizen, who is more than eighteen and less than forty-five years of age, and shall be divided into two classes—the organized militia, to be known as the National Guard of the State, Territory, or District of Columbia, or by such other designations as may be given them by the laws of the respective States or Territories, and the remainder to be known as the Reserve Militia."

Congress defines the militia in Title 10, United States Code, Chapter 13—The Militia. Under Section 311—Militia, it states:

Composition and classes

(a) The militia of the United States consists of all able-bodied males at least 17 years of age and...under 45 years of age who are, or who have made a declaration of intention to become, citizens of the United States and of female citizens of the United States who are members of the National Guard.
(b) The classes of the militia are —
  (1) the organized militia, which consists of the National Guard and the Naval Militia; and
  (2) the "unorganized militia" which consists of the members of the militia who are not members of the armed XX

Thus, if you are an able-bodied male citizen between the ages of 17 to 45, you are a member of the militia of the *United States!* In other words, both are classes of the *federal* militia—not a State militia organized to protect from federal tyranny. As we've already seen, Article I, Section 8, clause 15, 16 of the U.S. Constitution effectively took away the state militias by giving ultimate control to the federal government. The Dick Act and Title 10 completed the transfer by assigning all   able-bodied adult males into the "unorganized" *federal* militia. The organized militia, known as the National Guard of the United States (aka the army wearing another hat), is essentially loaned to the states until needed anywhere in the world. Hence, the ability to deploy the "National Guard" to Iraq and elsewhere as an "International Guard."

PART IV

BAN ASSAULT BANANAS

> The great masses of the people will more easily fall victims to a big lie than to a small one.
> — *Adolf Hitler*

Will Tyranny Happen Here?

Lord Action said in 1887 that "Power tends to corrupt and absolute power corrupts absolutely." Since all military power is now in the hands of the federal government, what will happen when all private citizens are eventually disarmed and helpless to resist?

We know that we can't rely on the Constitution to prevent tyranny — the courts routinely ignore that musty piece of parchment. Here's what a former Justice of the Supreme Court had to say:

> "The Constitution as many of us understood it, the Constitution that has meant so much to us, is gone. The guarantees that men and women have supposed protected them against arbitrary action have been swept away."
> - Justice McReynolds, *dissenting in a 1935 decision removing gold backing for the Dollar.*

More recently, Supreme Court Justice Antonin Scalia lamented that "Day by day, case by case, the Supreme Court is writing a new Constitution I no longer recognize."

Over the years many other Justices have likewise complained that the Supreme Court has interpreted away the entire Bill of Rights. It doesn't take an Einstein to understand why Oliver Wendell Holmes called the Supreme Court "Nine scorpions in a bottle" more than 50 years ago. When even Justices of the highest Court in the land are admitting that we have no real constitutional protections left, something is seriously wrong — tyranny not only can happen, it has happened. Perhaps we should take a closer look at things before we dutifully surrender and register our guns.

One of the most scholarly examinations of what is happening in America was made by Dr. Leonard Piekoff in his landmark book, *The Ominous Parallels: The End of Freedom in America.* Professor Piekoff traces the cause of Nazism and notes the similarities between America today and Germany before and during Hitler's reign. He warned back in 1982 in his book that America was moving toward an oligarchical dictatorship—an American version of Hitler's National Socialist Party dictatorship.

We've traveled a very long way toward Nazism since 1982, and especially since 9/11. For now, it only needs to be said that the key elements of Nazism/Fascism are already in place: militarism, national socialism, surveillance of citizens, heavy regulation of private enterprise, suppression of opposition, denial of individual rights, and strict gun control.

Hitler's Gun Control Laws Transplanted in America

I can't think of a more ominous warning, or a more certain coup de grâce, than the day Hitler's gun control laws are transplanted in America. Sadly, it's already happened but for most people nothing happens unless they hear it on CNN.

An organization called Jews for the Preservation of Firearms Ownership (JPFO) published their expose entitled *GUN CONTROL: Gateway to Tyranny* in 1993. Therein, authors Jay Simkin and Aaron Zelman provide definitive proof that Hitler's Nazi Weapons

BAN ASSAULT BANANAS

Law of March 18, 1938 was imposed on America in 1968.

JPFO's book contains the original German text of Hitler's 1938 law, along with a translation into English and a side—by—side paragraph comparison to the amended U.S. Gun Control Act of 1968 (GCA '68). The similarities of both laws include:

- Firearms dealers in Nazi Germany were required to record the "acquisition or disposal" of their firearms in a bound "Firearms Dealers Book." Here in the USA, it's a bound *"Firearms and Disposition Record" book.*
- Under GCA '68, purchasers are required to fill out an ATF Form 4473 - Firearms Transaction Record, and to sign under penalty of perjury that they are not legally barred from acquiring a firearm. *This form demands almost identical information and the same sworn statement as the Nazi Firearms Acquisition Permit.*
- Under both laws the government can decide what type of firearms citizens are allowed to purchase.
- Both laws allow an undefined "sporting purpose" criteria to be used for import restrictions.
- Both provide special exemptions for muzzle-loading and antique rifles (manufactured before 1870 under Nazi law, and before 1898 under GCA '68).
- Both have exemptions for non-projectile firearms, such as tear gas, pyrotechnics, and noise-makers such as starter pistols.
- Both laws have the same 18-year minimum age limit to purchase a rifle.

- Hitler's law required dealers to retain records for 10 years; U.S. law requires 20 years.
- Both laws require that records be open for inspection by the authorities at all times.
- Both also require that dealer records be surrendered to the authorities when a dealer goes out of business.

Can any rational person now believe that the similarities between Hitler's 1938 Weapons Law and the Gun Control Act of 1968 are mere coincidences? But just in case someone reading this needs more proof, let's first examine what was afoot in Congress prior to enactment of GCA 68.

Senator Thomas J. Dodd (D-Ct), now deceased, was chairman of the Senate Judiciary Subcommittee to Investigate Juvenile Delinquency. In June and July of 1968 he also chaired several hearings on related gun control bills: (1) to require registration of firearms (S—3604); to disarm lawless persons (S-3634); and to establish a National Firearms Registry (S-3637).

These bills were subsequently incorporated into GCA '68—but they were not original ideas: The ideas came from Hitler. Put simply, Congress copied Hitler's statutes, which would surely please Hitler himself, and definitely pleased all the gun control zealots who lauded GCA '68.

The confirming evidence was reprinted in JPFO's publication, which included a July 12, 1968 letter from a law librarian at the Library of Congress to Senator Dodd. The letter was in a package returning a copy of the original German text of Hitler's Weapons Law — text which Senator Dodd had submitted to the Library for translation into English.

BAN ASSAULT BANANAS

THE LIBRARY OF CONGRESS
Washington, D.C., July 12, 1968
HON. THOMAS J. DODD

Chairman, Special Subcommittee To Investigate Juvenile Delinquency, U.S. Senate, Washington, D.C.

DEAR SENATOR DODD:

Your request of July 2, 1968, addressed to the Legislative Reference Service, for the translation of several German laws has been referred to the Law Library for attention.

In compliance with your request and with reference to several telephone conversations between Miss Frank of your Office and Mr. Fred Karpf, European Law Division, we are enclosing herewith a translation of the Law on Weapons of March 18, 1938, prepared by Dr. William Solyom-Fekete of that Division, as well as the Xerox copy of the original German text which you supplied.

The translation of the Decree implementing the Law on weapons of March 19, 1938, and the pertinent provisions of the federal Hunting Law of March 30, 1961, is in preparation and will be sent to you as soon as completed,

Sincerely yours,
LEWIS C. COFFIN
Law Librarian

BAN ASSAULT BANANAS

This letter proves that Senator Dodd had a copy of Hitler's Law on Weapons at least four months before enactment of GCA '68 and we see what resulted. Of course many other major gun control bills have been passed since that time, and more are planned. Give the government an inch and they'll take a light-year.

After the publication of JPFO's revealing expose, members of Congress were sent copies to make them aware that Hitler's law was cloned and imposed on Americans. But Congress still has not repealed Hitler's Gun Control Act of 1968.

While GCA '68 doesn't include every restriction in the Nazi Weapons Law, certain cities and states have filled in the blanks, some have banned the sale and possession of certain firearms. It should be further noted that the punishment for almost all violations of Hitler's weapons Law was limited to 3 years imprisonment. The contrasting punishment for most U.S. gun law violations ranges from 10-30 years imprisonment—far harsher than even Hitler thought proper.

Hitler's gun control laws were enforced in Nazi Germany by a national police force known as the Gestapo—the Ge(heime) Sta(ats) Po(lizei). The same gun laws copied directly from Hitler's laws are enforced in this country by a national police force known as the BATFE—the Bureau of Alcohol, Tobacco, Firearms and Explosives (formerly BATF).

The popular delusion is that gun control laws are implemented to protect citizens, when in fact they are enacted to protect the government from the citizens. Politicians couldn't care less about you, except as sheep to fleece. We must always remember that gun control laws in Nazi Germany enabled the government to slaughter millions of *unarmed* men, women and children—Christians, Jews, Gypsies, and others. Think it can't happen here?

The Waco Massacre

After the federal government machine-gunned and burned alive 86 men, women, and children at Waco, Texas, Rep. John Dingell (D-MI) compared it to the Nazi massacre in Warsaw, Poland. In a newspaper opinion, Dingell wrote that in *both* massacres the attackers wore military-style clothing, jackboots, coal-scuttle helmets, and carried German-made machine guns.

Other similarities: The 2,000 Wehrmacht troops used tanks to slaughter an outcast group of religious Jews in the Warsaw Ghetto who were prohibited from owning firearms. Likewise with the Branch Davidians at Waco: an outcast group of religious believers residing in a ghetto-style building who were prohibited from owning certain firearms.

There is a most revealing dichotomy in the psyche of the American people in regards to the events at Waco. On the one hand most acknowledge that the Warsaw massacre was done by murderous government thugs. At the same time, and in classic Orwellian double-think, they simultaneously argue that the Waco massacre was a "justifiable culling" by well-meaning, albeit bumbling, "government "heroes." The rhetoric at that time was to call the Davidians "the Wackos at Waco."

Despite the bloody history of enforcing unconstitutional firearms laws in America (Waco, Ruby Ridge, and other lesser known events), Congress continues to permit Hitler's Weapons Law and others to remain on the books. In doing so, they are committing a crime against Americans, and are ignoring the sacrifices of 384,402 brave Americans who died during WWII alone to keep America free from Nazism (and the totalitarian rule of Japan).

Of course Hitler didn't have to contend with a Second Amendment to impose his 1938 Weapons Law. He simply ruled by decree without pretending to be anything other than a Nazi.

In this sense he was more honest than our politicians and judges who rule by decree when they conspire to enact and uphold Nazi laws that blatantly infringe on the Second Amendment.

PART V

"When Congress today wants to regulate something not authorized by the Constitution, it bows to the doctrine of enumerated powers by claiming that the thing it is regulating 'affects' commerce."
—*Roger Pilon,* "Restoring Constitutional Government"

The Interstate Commerce Scam

Although the courts have interpreted away the Second Amendment, and effectively all the others, the fact remains that the federal government has no authority to enforce its unconstitutional firearms laws within the states. This is because, unlike States, the federal government has only those powers that were *delegated* to it by the people—and specifically *enumerated* in the Constitution.

This limitation on federal power is set forth in the Constitution, immediately after the preamble, under Article I, Section One:

> "All legislative Powers *herein granted* shall be invested in a Congress..." (emphasis added).

This phrase was still not enough for the Ratifying States; they demanded a Tenth Amendment to make this limitation of power perfectly clear:

> "The powers not delegated to the United States by the Constitution nor prohibited by it to the States, are reserved to the States respectively, or to the people."

At no time has even the Supreme Court disputed that the Constitution created a federal government with strictly limited powers: See *Chisholm v. Georgia*, 1 L. Ed. 440 (1793) ("Each State in the Union is sovereign as to all powers reserved. It must necessarily be so because the United States have no claim to authority but such as the States have surrendered to them."); *New York v. United States*, 120 L.Ed. 2d 120 (1992).

("[N]o one disputes the proposition that '[t]he Constitution created a Federal government of limited powers.'") (quoting *Gregory v. Ashcroft*, 501 U.S. 452, 457 (1991)).

Most of the powers that were delegated to the federal government are enumerated in clauses under Article I, Section 8 of the Constitution. Even the power "[t]o make all Laws which shall be necessary and proper for carrying into Execution the foregoing Powers" that were delegated *must be enumerated.*

Unfortunately, as the anti-Federalists predicted, today there is almost no aspect of one's personal behavior or business activities that the federal government doesn't regulate, criminalize, or surreptitiously monitor. It's impossible to square this fact with the concept of limited federal powers.

So how does the federal government claim to have these non-delegated powers? In the case of firearms and most of the criminal laws, including drug possession, the Supreme Court simply crafted an expansive and deliberate misinterpretation of the delegated power to regulate interstate commerce (Article I, Section 8, Clause 3 of the Constitution).

Under their treasonous interpretation, any activity which the government wants to regulate or criminalize doesn't even have to be a "commercial" activity, nor does the activity have to be "interstate." The Supreme Court has determined that Congress can regulate anything that may *affect* interstate commerce—including personal behavior occurring wholly within a State!

By 1995, this perversion of the Constitution was becoming much too transparent for even the easily duped masses. Accordingly, the Supreme Court granted certiorari in the case of *United States v.*

BAN ASSAULT BANANAS

Lopez, 131 L. Ed. 2d 626 (1995) to "update" their excuses for 60-years of unconstitutional Interstate Commerce Clause jurisprudence. The Lopez case dealt with a federal law called the Gun-Free School Zones Act in 1990 that prohibited possession of a firearm within 1000 feet of a school.

To appear reasonable, by *slightly* limiting the expanded commerce clause, they struck down the 1990 Gun-Free School Zones Act. Their ruling was that firearms possession within 1000 feet of a school did not "substantially" affect interstate commerce.

In a concurring opinion, Justice Clarence Thomas pointed out that the Constitution never delegated the power to regulate *any* activity *within the States,* regardless of its effects on interstate commerce —substantial or otherwise—pursuant to the interstate commerce clause:

> "While the principal dissent concedes that there are limits to federal power, the sweeping nature of our current [substantial effects] test enables the dissent to argue that Congress can regulate gun possession. But it seems to me that the power to regulate "commerce" can by no means encompass authority over mere gun possession, any more than it empowers the Federal Government to regulate marriage, littering, or cruelty to animals throughout the 50 States. Our Constitution quite properly leaves such matters to the individual States, notwithstanding these activities' effects on interstate commerce...
>
> "After all, if Congress may regulate all matters that substantially affect commerce, there is no need for the Constitution to specify that Congress may enact bankruptcy laws, cl. 4, or coin money

and fix the standard of weights and measures, cl. 5, or punish counterfeiters of United States coin and Securities, cl. 6...

"Put simply, much if not all of Art. I, §8 (including portions of the Commerce Clause itself) would be surplusage if Congress had been given authority over matters that substantially affect interstate commerce. An interpretation of that makes the rest of §8 superfluous simply cannot be correct. Yet this Court's commerce clause jurisprudence has endorsed just such an interpretation: the power that we have accorded Congress has swallowed Art. I, §8."

APPENDIX

The great object is that every man be armed.
— *Patrick Henry*

Speeches of Patrick Henry
(June 5 and 7, 1788)

The following two speeches from Patrick Henry were first printed in a 1788-1789 Petersburg, Virginia edition of the "Debates and other Proceedings of the Virginia Convention of 1788." Here, Patrick Henry argues against an all-powerful central Government. Most of his dire predictions for the loss of liberty came true.

5 June 1788

Mr. Chairman I rose yesterday to ask a question which arose in my own mind. When I asked that question, I thought the meaning of my interrogation was obvious: The fate of this question and of America may depend on this: Have they said, we, the States? Have they made a proposal of a compact between states? If they had, this would be a confederation: It is otherwise most clearly a consolidated Government. The question turns, Sir, on that poor little thing-the expression, *We, the people,* instead of the States, of America. I need not take much pains to show that the principles of this system are extremely pernicious, impolitic, and dangerous. Is this a monarchy, like England-a compact between prince and people, with checks on the former to secure the liberty of the latter? Is this a Confederacy, like Holland-an association of a number of independent states, each of which retains its individual sovereignty? It is not a democracy, wherein the people retain all their rights securely. Had these principles been adhered to, we should not have been brought to this alarming transition, from a Confederacy to a consolidated I. We have no detail of these great consideration, which, in my opinion, ought to have abounded before we should recur to a Government of this kind. Here is a revolution as radical as that which separated us from Great Britain. It is radical in this transition; our rights and privileges are endangered, and the sovereignty of the states will be relinquished: And cannot we plainly see that this is actually the case? The rights of conscience, trial by jury, liberty of the press, all your immunities and franchises, all pretensions to human rights and privileges, are rendered insecure, if not lost, by this change, so loudly talked of by some, and inconsiderately by others. Is this tame relinquishment of rights worthy of freemen? Is it worthy of that manly fortitude that ought to characterize republicans; It is said eight States have adopted this plan. I declare that if twelve States and a half had adopted it, I would, with manly firmness, and in spite of an erring world, reject it. You are not to inquire how your trade may be increased, nor how you are to become a great and powerful people, but how your liberties can be secured; for liberty ought to be the direct end of your I. Having premised these things, I shall, with the aid of my judgment and information, which, I confess, are not extensive. go into the discussion of this system more minutely. Is it necessary for your liberty that you should abandon those great rights by the adoption of this system? Is the relinquishment of the trial by jury and the liberty of the press necessary for your liberty? Will the abandonment of your most sacred rights tend to the security of your liberty? Liberty, the greatest of all earthly blessings give us that precious jewel, and you may take every thing else: But I am fearful I have lived long enough to become an fellow: Perhaps an

BAN ASSAULT BANANAS

invincible attachment to the dearest rights of man, may, in these refined, enlightened days, be deemed old fashioned: If so, I am contented to be so: I say, the time has been when every pore of my heart beat for American liberty, and which, I believe, had a counterpart in the breast of every true American: But suspicions have gone forth-suspicions of my integrity-publicly reported that my professions are not real. 23 years ago was I supposed a traitor to my country; I was then said to be the bane of sedition, because I supported the rights of my country: I may be thought suspicious when I say our privileges and rights are in danger. But, Sir, a number of the people of this country are weak enough to think these things are too true: I am happy to find that the Honorable Gentleman on the other side declares they are groundless: But, Sir, suspicion is a virtue, as long as its object is the preservation of the public good, and as long as it stays within proper bounds: Should it fall on me, I am contented: Conscious rectitude is a powerful consolation: I trust there are many who think my professions for the public good to be real. Let your suspicion look to both sides: There are many on the other side, who possibly may have been persuaded of the necessity of these measures. which I conceive to be dangerous to your liberty.

Guard with jealous attention the public liberty. Suspect every one who approaches that jewel. Unfortunately, nothing will preserve it but downright force: Whenever you give up that force, you are inevitably ruined, I am answered by gentlemen, that though I might speak of terrors, yet the fact was, that we were surrounded by none of the dangers apprehended. I conceive this new Government to be one of those dangers: It has produced those horrors which distress many of our best citizens.

We are come hither to preserve the poor commonwealth of Virginia, if it can be possibly done: Something must be done to preserve your liberty and mine: The Confederation; this same despised Government, merits, in my opinion, the highest encomium: It carried us through a long and dangerous war: It rendered us victorious in that bloody conflict with a powerful nation: It has secured us a territory greater than any European monarch possesses: And shall a government which has been thus strong and vigorous, be accused of imbecility and abandoned for want of energy? Consider what you are about to do before you part with this Government. Take longer time in reckoning things: Revolutions like this have happened in almost every country in Europe: Similar examples are to be found in ancient Greece and ancient Rome: Instances of the people losing their liberty by their carelessness and the ambition of a few. We are cautioned by the Honorable Gentleman who presides, against faction and turbulence: I acknowledge that licentiousness is dangerous, and that it ought to be provided against: I acknowledge also the new form of Government may effectually prevent it: Yet, there is another thing it will as effectually do: it will oppress and ruin the people. There are sufficient guards placed against sedition and licentiousness: For when power is given to this Government to suppress these, or, for any other purpose, the language it assumes is clear, express, and unequivocal; but when this Constitution speaks of privileges, there is an ambiguity, Sir, a fatal ambiguity;-an ambiguity which is very astonishing: In the clause under consideration, there is the strangest language that I can conceive. I mean, when it says that there shall not be more Representatives than one for every 30,000. Now, Sir, how easy is it to evade this privilege? "The number shall not exceed one for every 30,000." This may be satisfied by one Representative from each State. Let our numbers be ever so great, this immense continent. may, by this artful expression, be reduced to have but 13 Representatives: I confess this construction is not natural; but the ambiguity of the expression lays a good ground for a quarrel. Why was it not clearly and unequivocally expressed, that they should be entitled, to have one for every 30,000? This would have obviated all disputes; and was this difficult to be done?

What is the inference? When population increases, and a state shall send Representatives in this proportion, Congress may remand them, because the right of having one for every 30,000 is not clearly expressed: this possibility of reducing the number to one for each state approximates to probability by that other expression, "but each state shall at least have one Representative." Now, is it not clear that, from the first expression, the number might be reduced so much that some States should have no Representatives at all, were it not for the insertion of this last expression? And as this is the only restriction upon them, we may fairly conclude that they may restrain the number to one from each State: Perhaps the same horrors may hang over my mind again. I shall be told I am continually afraid: But, Sir, I have strong cause of apprehension: In some parts of the plan before you, the great rights of freemen are endangered, in other parts absolutely taken away. How does your trial by jury stand? In civil cases gone-not sufficiently secured in criminal-this best

BAN ASSAULT BANANAS

privilege is gone: But we are told that we need not fear; because those in power, being our Representatives, will not abuse the power we put in their hands: I am not well versed in history, but I will submit to your recollection, whether liberty has been destroyed most often by the licentiousness of the people, or by the tyranny of rulers? I imagine, sir, you will find the balance on the side of tyranny: Happy will you be if you miss the fate of those nations. who, omitting to resist their oppressors. or negligently suffering their liberty to be wrested from them, have groaned under intolerable despotism. Most of the human race are now in this deplorable condition: And those nations who have gone in search of grandeur, power. and splendor, have also fallen a sacrifice, and been the victims of their own folly: While they acquired those visionary blessings, they lost their freedom. My great objection to this Government is, that it does not leave us the means of defending our rights, or cf waging war against tyrants: It is urged by some gentlemen, that this new plan will bring us an acquisition of strength, an army, and the militia of the States: This is an idea extremely ridiculous: Gentlemen cannot be earnest.

This acquisition will trample on our fallen liberty: Let my beloved Americans guard against that fatal lethargy that has pervaded the universe: Have we the means of resisting disciplined armies, when our only defence, the militia, is put into the hands of Congress? The Honorable Gentleman said, that great danger would ensue if the Convention rose without adopting this system: I ask, Where is that danger? I see none: Other Gentlemen have told us within these walls, that the Union is gone-or, that the Union will be gone: Is not this trifling with the judgment of their

BAN ASSAULT BANANAS

fellow-citizens? Till they tell us the grounds of their fears, I will consider them as imaginary: I rose to make inquiry where those dangers were: they could make no answer: I believe I never shall have that answer: Is there a disposition in the people of this country to revolt against the dominion of laws? Has there been a single tumult in Virginia? Have not the people of Virginia, when laboring under the severest pressure of accumulated distresses, manifested the most cordial acquiescence in the execution of the laws'? What could be more awful than their unanimous acquiescence under general distresses? Is there any revolution in Virginia?

Whither is the spirit of America gone? Whither is the genius of America fled? It was but yesterday, when our enemies marched in triumph through our country. Yet the people of this country could not be appalled by their pompous armaments: They stopped their career, and victoriously captured them. Where is the peril, now, compared to that?

Some minds are agitated by foreign alarms: Happily for us. there is no real danger from Europe: that country is engaged in more arduous business: from that quarter there is no cause of fear: You may sleep in safety forever for them. Where is the danger? If, Sir, there was any, I would recur to the American spirit to defend us; that spirit which has enabled us to surmount the greatest difficulties: To that illustrious spirit l address my most fervent prayer, to prevent our adopting a system destructive to liberty. Let no Gentlemen be told, that it is not safe to reject this. Wherefore is it not safe? We are told there are dangers; but those dangers are ideal; they cannot be demonstrated: To encourage us to adopt it, they tell us that there is a plain, easy way of getting amendments: When I come to contemplate this part, I suppose that I am mad, or that my countrymen are so: The way to amendment is, in my conception, shut. Let us consider this plain, easy way: "The Congress, whenever two thirds of both Houses shall deem it necessary, shall propose amendments to this Constitution, or, on the application of the Legislatures of two thirds of the several states, shall call a Convention for proposing amendments, which, in either case, shall be valid to all intents and purposes, as part of this Constitution, when ratified by the Legislatures of three-fourths of the several States, or by the Conventions in three-fourths thereof, as the one or the other mode of ratification may be proposed by the Congress. Provided, that no amendment which may be made prior to the year 1808, shall in any manner affect the first and fourth clauses in the ninth section of the first article; and that no State, without its consent, shall be deprived of its equal suffrage in the Senate." Hence it appears that three-fourths of the States must ultimately agree to any amendments that may be necessary. Let us consider the consequence of this: However uncharitable it may appear, yet I must tell my opinion, that the most unworthy character may get into power, and prevent the introduction of amendments: Let us suppose (for the case is supposable, possible, and probable) that you happen to deal those powers to unworthy hands; will they relinquish powers already in their possession, or agree to amendments? Two-thirds of the Congress, or, of the State Legislatures, are necessary even to propose amendments: If one-third of these be unworthy men, they may prevent the application for amendments; but what is destructive and mischievous, is, that three-fourths of the State Legislatures, or of the State Conventions, must concur in the amendments when proposed: In such numerous bodies, there must necessarily be some designing bad men: To suppose that so large a number as three-fourths of the States will concur, is to suppose that they will possess genius, intelligence, and integrity, approaching to miraculous. It would indeed be miraculous that they should concur in the same amendments, or even in such as would bear some likeness to one another. For four of the smallest States, that do not collectively contain one-tenth part of the population of the United States, may obstruct the most salutary and necessary amendments: Nay, in these four States, six tenths of the people may reject these amendments; and suppose, that amendments shall be opposed to amendments (which is highly probable) is it possible, that three-fourths can ever agree to the same amendments? A bare majority in these four small States may hinder the adoption of amendments; so that we may fairly and justly conclude, that one-twentieth part of the American people, may prevent the removal of the most grievous inconveniences and oppression, by refusing to accede to amendments. A trifling minority may reject the most salutary amendments. Is this an easy mode of securing the public liberty? It is, Sir, a most fearful situation. when the most contemptible minority can prevent the alteration of the most oppressive Government; for it may, in many respects, prove to be such. Is this the spirit of republicanism? What, Sir, is the genius of democracy? Let me read that clause of the Bill of Rights of Virginia which relates to this: third clause. "That Government is or ought to be instituted for the common benefit, protection, and security of the people, nation, or community: Of all the various modes and forms of I. that is best which is capable of producing the greatest degree of happiness and safety, and is most effectually secured against the danger of mal-administration, and that whenever any I shall be found inadequate, or contrary to those purposes, a majority of the community hath, an indubitable, unalienable, and indefeasible right to reform, alter, or abolish it, in such manner as shall be judged most conducive to the public weal." This, Sir, is the language of democracy; that a majority of the community have a right to alter their Government when found to be oppressive: But how different is the genius of your new Constitution from this? How different from the sentiments of freemen, that a contemptible minority can prevent the good of the majority? If then Gentlemen standing on this ground, are come to that point, that they are willing to bind themselves and their posterity to be oppressed, 1 am amazed and inexpressibly astonished. If this be the opinion of the majority, I must submit; but to me, Sir, it appears perilous and destructive: I cannot help thinking so: Perhaps it may be the result of my age; these may be feelings natural to a man of my years, when the American spirit has left him, and his mental powers, like the members of the body, are decayed. If, Sir, amendments are left to the twentieth or tenth part of the people of America, your liberty is gone forever. We have heard that there is a great deal of bribery practiced in the House of Commons in England; and that many of the members raised themselves to preferments. by selling the rights of the people: But, Sir, the tenth pan of that body cannot continue oppressions on the rest of the people.

BAN ASSAULT BANANAS

English liberty is in this case, on a firmer foundation than American liberty. It will be easily contrived to procure the opposition of one tenth of the people to any alteration, however judicious. The Honorable Gentleman who presides, told us, that to prevent abuses in our I, we will assemble in Convention, recall our delegated powers, and punish our servants for abusing the trust reposed in them. Oh, Sir, we should have fine times indeed, if to punish tyrants, it were only sufficient to assemble the people. Your arms wherewith you could defend yourselves, are gone; and you have no longer an aristocratical; no longer democratical spirit. Did you ever read of any revolution in a nation, brought about by the punishment of those in power. inflicted by those who had no power at all'? You read of a riot act in a country which is called one of the freest in the world, where a few neighbors cannot assemble without the risk of being shot by a hired soldiery, the engines of despotism. We may see such an act in America.

A standing army we shall have also, to execute the execrable commands of tyranny: And how are you to punish them'? Will you order them to be punished? Who shall obey these orders? Will your Mace-bearer be a match for a disciplined regiment? [n What situation are we to be? The clause before you gives a power of direct taxation, unbounded and unlimited: Exclusive power of Legislation in all cases whatsoever, for ten miles square; and over all places purchased for the erection of forts. magazines, arsenals, dockyards, etc. What resistance could be made? The attempt would be madness. You will find all the strength of this country in the hands of your enemies: Those garrisons will naturally be the strongest places in the country. Your militia is given up to Congress also in another part of this plan: They will therefore act as they think proper: All power will be in their own possession: You cannot force them to receive their punishment: Of what service would militia be to you, when most probably you will not have a single musket in the State; for as arms are to be provided by Congress, they may or may not furnish them. Let me here call your attention to that part which gives the Congress power, *"To provide for organizing, arming, and disciplining the militia, and for governing such part of them as may be employed in the service of the United States, reserving to the States respectively, the appointment of the officers, and the authority of training the militia, according to the discipline prescribed by Congress." By this, Sir, you see that their control over our last and best defence is unlimited. If they neglect or refuse to discipline or arm our militia, they will be useless: the States can do neither, this power being exclusively given to Congress: The power of appointing officers over men not disciplined or armed is ridiculous: So that this pretended little remains of power left to the States may, at the pleasure of Congress, be rendered nugatory. Our situation will be deplorable indeed: Nor can we ever expect to get this Government amended, since I have already shewn, that a very small minority may prevent it; and that small minority interested in the continuance of the oppression: Will the oppressor let go the oppressed? Was there even an instance? Can the annals of mankind exhibit one single example, where rulers overcharged with power willingly let go the oppressed, though solicited and requested most earnestly? The application for amendments will therefore be fruitless. (Emphasis added)*

BAN ASSAULT BANANAS

Sometimes the oppressed have got loose by one of those bloody struggles that desolate a country. A willing relinquishment of power is one of those things which human nature never was, nor ever will be capable of: The Honorable Gentleman's observations respecting the people's fight of being the agents in the formation of this Government, are not accurate in my humble conception. The distinction between a National Government and a Confederacy is not sufficiently discerned. Had the delegates who were sent to Philadelphia a power to propose a Consolidated Government instead of a Confederacy? Were they not deputed by States, and not by the people? The assent of the people in their collective capacity is not necessary to the formation of a Federal Government.

The people have no right to enter into leagues, alliances, or confederations: They are not the proper agents for this purpose: States and sovereign powers are the only proper agents for this kind of Government: Shew me an instance where the people have exercised this business: Has it not always gone through the Legislatures? I refer you to the treaties with France, Holland, and other nations: How were they made? Were they not made by the States? Are the people therefore in their aggregate capacity, the proper persons to form a Confederacy? This, therefore, ought to depend on the consent of the Legislatures; the people having never sent delegates to make any proposition for changing the Government. Yet I must say, at the same time, that it was made on grounds the most pure, and perhaps I might have been brought to consent to it so far as to the change of Government ; but there is one thing in it which I never would acquiesce in. I mean the

BAN ASSAULT BANANAS

changing it into a Consolidated Government; which is so abhorrent in my mind. The Honorable Gentleman then went on tot he figure we make with foreign nations; the contemptible one we make in France and Holland; which, according to the substance of my notes, he attributes to the present feeble Government. An opinion has gone forth, we find, that we are a contemptible people: The time has been when we were thought otherwise: Under the same despised Government, we commanded the respect of all Europe: Wherefore are we now reckoned otherwise? The American spirit has fled from hence: It has gone to regions, where it has never been expected: It has gone to the people of France in search of a splendid Government-a strong energetic Government. Shall we imitate the example of those nations who have gone from
a simple to a splendid Government? Are those nations more worthy of our imitation? What can make an adequate satisfaction to them for the loss they have suffered in attaining such a Government for the loss of their liberty? If we admit this Consolidated Government it will be because we like a great splendid one. Some way or other we must be a great and mighty empire; we must have an army, and a navy, and a number of things: When the American spirit was in its youth, the language of America was different: Liberty, Sir, was then the primary object. We are descended from a people whose Government was founded on liberty: Our glorious forefathers of Great-Britain, made liberty the foundation of every thing. That country is become a great, mighty, and splendid nation; not because their Government is strong and energetic; but, Sir, because liberty is its direct end and foundation: We drew the spirit of

liberty from our British ancestors; by that spirit we have triumphed over every difficulty: But now, Sir, the American spirit, assisted by the ropes and chains of consolidation, is about to convert this country to a powerful and mighty empire: If you make the citizens of this country agree to become the subjects of one great consolidated empire of America, your Government will not have sufficient energy to keep them together: Such a Government is incompatible with the genius of republicanism: There will be no checks, no real balances. in this Government: What can avail your specious imaginary balances, your rope-dancing, chain-rattling, ridiculous ideal checks and contrivances? But, Sir, we are not feared by foreigners: we do not make nations tremble: Would this, Sir, constitute happiness. or secure liberty? I trust, Sir, our political hemisphere will ever direct their operations to the security of those objects. Consider our situation, Sir: Go to the poor man, ask him what he does; he will inform you, that he enjoys the fruits of his labour, under his own fig-tree, with his wife and children around him, in peace and security. Go to every other member of society, you will find the same tranquil ease and content; you will find no alarms or disturbances: Why then tell us of dangers to terrify us into an adoption of this new Government? And yet who knows the dangers that this new system may produce; they are out of the sight of the common people: They cannot foresee latent consequences: I dread the operation of it on the middling and lower classes of people: It is for them I fear the adoption of this system. I fear I tire the patience of the Committee, but I beg to be indulged with a few more observations: When I thus profess myself an advocate for the liberty of the people, I shall be told, I am a designing man, that I am to be a great man, that I am to be a demagogue; and many similar illiberal insinuations will be thrown out; but, Sir, conscious rectitude, out-weighs those things with me: I see great jeopardy in this new Government. I see none from our present one: I hope some Gentleman or other will bring forth, in full array, those dangers, if there be any, that we may see and touch them.

7 June 1788

I have thought, and still think, that a full investigation of the actual situation of America ought to precede any decision of this great and important question. That Government is no more than a choice among evils, is acknowledged by the most intelligent among mankind, and has been a standing maxim for ages. If it be demonstrated that the adoption of the new plan is a little or a trifling evil, then, Sir, I acknowledge that adoption ought to follow: But, Sir, if this be a truth that its adoption may entail misery on the free people of this country, I then insist that rejection ought to follow. Gentlemen strongly urge its adoption will be a mighty benefit to us: But, Sir, I am made of such incredulous materials that assertions and declarations, do not satisfy me. I must be convinced, Sir. I shall retain my infidelity on that subject, till I see our liberties secured in a manner perfectly satisfactory to my understanding. You are told [by Governor Randolph] there is no peace, although you fondly flatter yourselves that all is peace--- No peace--- a general cry and alarm in the country --- Commerce, riches, and wealth, vanished--- Citizens going to seek comforts in other parts of the world --- Laws insulted -- Many instances of

BAN ASSAULT BANANAS

tyrannical legislation, These things, Sir, are new to me. He has made the discovery — As to the administration of justice, I believe that failures in commerce, etc. cannot be attributed to it. My age enables me to recollect its progress under the old Government. I can justify it by saying, that it continues in the same manner in this State, as it did under the former Government . As to other parts of the Continent, I refer that to other Gentlemen. As to the ability of those who administer it, I believe they would not suffer by a comparison with those who administered it under the royal authority. Where is the cause of complaint if the wealthy go away? Is this added to the other circumstances, of such enormity, and does it bring such danger over this Commonwealth as to warrant so important, and so awful a change in so precipitate a manner'? As to insults offered to the laws, I know of none. In this respect, I believe this Commonwealth would not suffer by a comparison with the former Government . The laws are as well executed, and as patiently acquiesced in, as they were under the royal administration. Compare the situation of the country - Compare that of our citizens to what they were then, and decide whether persons and property are not as safe and secure as they were at that time. Is there a man in this Commonwealth, whose person can be insulted with impunity'? Cannot redress be had here for personal insults or injuries, as well as in any part of the world - as well as in those countries where Aristocrats and Monarchs triumph and reign? Is not the protection of property in full operation here'? The contrary cannot with truth be charged on this Commonwealth. Those severe charges which are exhibited against it, appear to me totally groundless.

BAN ASSAULT BANANAS

On a fair investigation. we shall be found to be surrounded by no real dangers. We have the animating fortitude and persevering alacrity of republican men, to carry us through misfortunes and calamities. 'Tis the fortune of a republic to be able to withstand the stormy ocean of human vicissitudes. I know of no danger awaiting us. Public and private security are to be found here in the highest degree. Sir, it is the fortune of a free people, not to be intimidated by imaginary dangers. Fear is the passion of slaves. Our political and natural hemisphere are now equally tranquil. Let us recollect the awful magnitude of the subject of our deliberation.

Let us consider the latent consequences of an erroneous decision--- and let not our minds be led away by unfair misrepresentations and uncandid suggestions. There have been many instances of uncommon lenity and temperance used in the exercise of power in this Commonwealth. I could call your recollection to many that happened during the war and since ---- But every Gentleman here must be apprized of them. ...I have said that I thought this a Consolidated Government: I will now prove it. Will the great rights of the people be secured by this Government? Suppose it should prove oppressive, how can it be altered?

Our Bill of Rights declares, "That a majority of the community hath an undubitable, unalienable, and indefeasible right to reform, alter, or abolish it, in such manner as shall be judged most conducive to the public weal." I have just proved that one tenth, or less, of the people of America, a most despicable minority may prevent this reform or alteration. Suppose the people of Virginia should wish to alter their Government; can a majority of them do it? No, because they are connected with other men; or, in other words, consolidated with other States: When the people of Virginia at a future day shall wish to alter their Government , though they should be unanimous in this desire, yet they may be prevented there from by a despicable minority at the extremity of the United States: The founders of your own Constitution made your Government changeable: But the power of changing it is gone from you! Whither is it gone? It is placed in the same hands that hold the rights of twelve other States; and those who hold those rights have right and power to keep them: It is not the particular Government of Virginia: One of the leading features of that Government is, that a majority can alter it, when necessary for the public good. This Government is not a Virginian but an American Government . Is it not therefore, a Consolidated Government? The sixth clause of your Bill of Rights tells you, "That elections of members to serve as Representatives of the people in Assembly, ought to be free, and that all men having sufficient evidence of permanent common interest with, and attachment to the community, have the right of suffrage, and cannot be taxed or deprived of their property for public uses, without their own consent, or that of their Representatives so elected, nor bound by any law to which they have not in like manner assented for the public good."

But what does this Constitution say? The clause under consideration gives an unlimited and unbounded power of taxation: Suppose every delegate from Virginia opposes a law laying a tax, what will it avail'? They are opposed by a majority: Eleven members can destroy their efforts: Those feeble ten cannot prevent the passing the most oppressive tax law. So that in direct opposition to the spirit and express language of your Declaration of Rights, you are taxed not by your own consent, but by people who have no connection with you. The next clause of the Bill of Rights tells you, "That all power of suspending law, or the execution of laws, by any authority without the consent of the Representatives of the people, is injurious to their rights, and ought not to be exercised." This tells us that there can be no suspension of Government , or laws without our own consent: Yet this Constitution can counteract and suspend any of our laws, that contravene its oppressive operation; for they have the power of direct taxation; which suspends our Bill of Rights; and it is expressly provided, that they can make all laws necessary for carrying their powers into execution; and it is declared paramount to the laws and constitutions of the States. Consider how the only remaining defence we have left is destroyed in this manner. Besides the expenses of maintaining the Senate and other House in as much splendor as they please, there is to be a great and mighty President, with very extensive powers; the powers of a King: He is to be supported in extravagant magnificence: So that the whole of our property may be taken by this American Government , by laying what taxes they please, giving themselves what salaries they please, and suspending our laws at their pleasure: I might be thought too inquisitive, but I believe I should take up but very little of your time in enumerating the little power that is left to the Government of Virginia; for this power is reduced to little or nothing: Their garrisons, magazines, arsenals, and forts, which will be situated in the strongest places within the States:

Their ten miles square, with all the fine ornaments of human life, added to their powers, and taken from the States, will reduce the power of the latter to nothing. The voice of tradition, I trust, will inform posterity of our struggles for freedom: If our descendants be worthy the name of Americans, they will preserve. and hand down to their latest posterity, the transactions of the present times; and though, l confess, my exclamations are not worthy the hearing, they will see that I have done my utmost to preserve their liberty: For I never will give up the power of direct taxation, but for a scourge: l am willing to give it conditionally; that is, alter non-compliance with requisitions. I will do more, Sir, and what I hope will convince the most skeptical man, that I am a lover of the American Union, that in case Virginia shall not make punctual payment, the control of our custom houses, and the whole regulation of trade, shall be given to Congress, and that Virginia shall depend on Congress even for passports, till Virginia shall have paid the last farthing; and furnished the last soldier: Nay, Sir. there is another alternative to which I would consent: Even that they should strike us out of the Union. and take away from us all federal privileges till we comply with federal requisitions; but let it depend upon our own pleasure to pay our money in the most easy manner for our people. Were all the States, more terrible than the mother country, to join against us, I hope Virginia could defend herself; but, Sir, the dissolution of the Union is most abhorrent to my mind: The first thing I have at heart is American liberty; the second thing is American Union; and I hope the people of Virginia will endeavor to preserve that Union: The increasing population of the southern States, is far greater than that of New-

BAN ASSAULT BANANAS

England: Consequently, in a short time, they will be far more numerous than the people of that country: Consider this, and you will find this State more particularly interested to support American liberty, and not bind our posterity by an improvident relinquishment of our rights. I would give the best security for a punctual compliance with requisitions; but I beseech Gentlemen, at all hazards, not to give up this unlimited power of taxation: The Honorable Gentleman has told us that these powers given to Congress, are accompanied by a Judiciary which will connect all: On examination you will find this very Judiciary oppressively constructed; your jury trial destroyed. and the Judges dependent on Congress. In this scheme of energetic Government, the people will find two sets of tax-gatherers—the State and the Federal Sheriffs. This it seems to me will produce such dreadful oppression, as the people cannot possibly bear: The Federal Sheriff may commit what oppression, make what distresses he pleases, and ruin you with impunity: For how are you to tie his hands? Have you any sufficiently decided means of preventing him from sucking your blood by speculations. commissions and fees? Thus thousands of your people will be most shamefully robbed: Our State Sheriffs, those unfeeling blood—suckers, have, under the watchful eye of our Legislature, committed the most horrid and barbarous ravages on our people: It has required the most constant vigilance of the Legislature to keep them from totally ruining the people: A repeated succession of laws has been made to suppress their iniquitous speculations and cruel extortions; and as often has their nefarious ingenuity devised methods of evading the force of those laws: In the struggle they have generally triumphed over the

BAN ASSAULT BANANAS

Legislature. It is a fact that lands have been sold for five shillings, which were worth one hundred pounds: If Sheriffs thus immediately under the eye of our State Legislature and Judiciary, have dared to commit these outrages. What would they not have done if their masters had been at Philadelphia or New York? If they perpetrate the most unwarrantable outrage on your person or property, you cannot get redress on this side of Philadelphia or New York: and how can you get it there? If your domestic avocations could permit you to go thither. there you must appeal to Judges sworn to support this Constitution, in opposition to that of any State, and who may also be inclined to favor their own officers: When these harpies are aided by excisemen, who may search at any time your houses and most secret recesses, will the people bear it? If you think so you differ from me: Where I thought there was a possibility of such mischief's, I would grant power with a niggardly hand; and here there is a strong probability that these oppressions shall actually happen. I may be told, that it is safe to err on that side; because such regulations may be made by Congress as shall restrain these officers, and because laws are made by our Representatives, and judged by righteous Judges: But, Sir, as these regulations may be made, so they may not; and many reasons there are to induce a belief that they will not: I shall therefore be an infidel on that point till the day of my death.

This Constitution is said to have beautiful features; but when I come to examine these features, Sir, they appear to me horribly frightful: Among other deformities, it has an awful squinting; it squints towards monarchy: And does not this raise indignation in the breast of every American? Your

BAN ASSAULT BANANAS

President may easily become King: Your Senate is so imperfectly constructed that your dearest rights may be sacrificed by what may be a small minority; and a very small minority may continue forever unchangeably this Government , although horridly defective: Where are your checks in this Government? Your strong holds will be in the hands of your enemies: It is on a supposition that our American Governors shall be honest, that all the good qualities of this Government are founded: But its defective, and imperfect construction, puts it in their power to perpetrate the worst of mischief's, should they be bad men: And, Sir, would not all the world, from the Eastern to the Western hemisphere, blame our distracted folly in resting our rights upon the contingency of our rulers being good or bad. Shew me that age and country where the rights and liberties of the people were placed on the sole chance of their rulers being good men, without a consequent loss of liberty? 1 say that the loss of that dearest privilege has ever followed with absolute certainty, every such mad attempt. lf your American chief, be a man of ambition, and abilities, how easy is it for him to render himself absolute: The army is in his hands, and, if he be a man of address, it will be attached to him; and it will be the subject of long meditation with him to seize the first auspicious moment to accomplish his design; and. Sir, will the American spirit solely relieve you when this happens? I would rather infinitely, and I am sure most of this Convention are of the same opinion, have a King, Lords, and Commons, than a Government so replete with such insupportable evils. If we make a King, we may prescribe the rules by which he shall rule his people, and interpose such checks as shall prevent him from infringing them: But the President, in the field, at the head of his army, can prescribe the terms on which he shall reign master, so far that it will puzzle any American ever to get his neck from under the galling yoke. I cannot with patience. think of this idea. If ever he violates the laws, one of two things will happen: He shall come at the head of his army to carry every thing before him; or, he will give bail, or do what Mr. Chief Justice will order him. If he be guilty, will not the recollection of his crimes teach him to make one bold push for the American throne? Will not the immense difference between being master of every thing, and being ignominiously tried and punished, powerfully excite him to make this bold push? But, Sir, where is the existing force to punish him? Can he not at the head of his army beat down every opposition? Away with your President. we shall have a King: The army will salute him Monarch; your militia will leave you and assist in making him King, and fight against you: And what have you to oppose this force'? What will then become of you and your rights? Will not absolute despotism ensue'? [Here Mr. Henry strongly and pathetically expatiated on the probability of the President's enslaving America and the horrid consequences that must result. What can be more defective than the clause concerning the elections? --- The control given to Congress over the time, place, and manner of holding elections, will totally destroy the end of suffrage. The elections may be held at one place, and the most inconvenient in the State; or they may be at remote distances from those who have a right of suffrage: Hence nine out often must either not vote at all, or vote for strangers: For the most influential characters will be applied to, to know who are the most proper to be chosen. I repeat, that the control of Congress over the manner, etc. of electing, well warrants this idea. The natural consequence will be, that this democratic branch, will possess none of the public confidence: The people will be prejudiced against Representatives chosen in such an injudicious manner. The proceedings in the northern conclave will be hidden from the yeomanry of this country: We are told that the yeas and nays shall be taken, and entered on the journals. This, Sir, will avail nothing: It may be locked up in their chests, and concealed forever from the people; for they are not to publish what parts they think require secrecy: They may think, and will think, the whole requires it. Another beautiful feature of this Constitution is the publication from time to time of the receipts and expenditures of the public money. This expression, from time to time, is very indefinite and indeterminate: It may extend to a century. Grant that any of them are wicked. they may squander the public money so as to ruin you, and yet this expression will give you no redress. I say, they may ruin you;--- for where, Sir, is the responsibility? The yeas and nays will shew you nothing, unless they be fools as well as knaves: For after having wickedly trampled on the rights of the people, they would act like fools indeed, were they to public and divulge their iniquity, when they have it equally in their power to suppress and conceal it. --- Where is the responsibility --- that leading principle in the British Government? In that government a punishment, certain and inevitable, is provided: But in this, there is no real actual punishment for the grossest maladministration. They may go without punishment, though they commit the most outrageous violation on our immunities. That paper may tell me they will be punished. I ask, by what law? They must make the law --- for there is no existing law to do it. What --- will they make a law to punish themselves? This, Sir, is my great objection to the Constitution, that there is no true responsibility -- and that the preservation of our liberty depends on the single chance of men being virtuous enough to make laws to punish themselves. In the country from which we are descended, they have real, and not imaginary, responsibility --- for there, maladministration has cost their heads, to some of the most saucy geniuses that ever were. The Senate, by making treaties may destroy your liberty and laws for want of responsibility. Two-thirds of those that shall happen to be present, can, with the President, make treaties, that shall be the supreme law of the land: They may make the most ruinous treaties; and yet there is no punishment for them. Whoever shows me a punishment provided for them, will oblige me. So, Sir, notwithstanding there are eight pillars, they want another. Where will they make another? I trust, Sir, the exclusion of the evils wherewith this system is replete, in its present form, will be made a condition, precedent to its adoption, by this or any other State. The transition from a general unqualified admission to offices, to a consolidation of Government , seems easy; for though the American States are dissimilar in their structure, this will assimilate Them: this, Sir, is itself a strong consolidating feature, and is not one of the least dangerous in that system. Nine states are sufficient to establish this Government over those nine. Imagine that nine have come into it. Virginia has certain scruples. Suppose she will consequently, refuse to join with those States: ---May not they still continue in friendship and union with her? If she sends her annual requisitions in dollars, do you think their stomachs will be so squeamish as to refuse her dollars? Will they not accept her regiments? They would intimidate you into an inconsiderate adoption, and frighten you with ideal evils, and that the Union shall be dissolved. 'Tis a bugbear, Sir:--- The fact is, Sir, that the eight adopting States can hardly stand on their own legs. Public fame tells us that the adopting States have already heart-burnings and animosity, and repent their precipitate hurry: This, Sir, may occasion exceeding great mischief. When I reflect on these and many other circumstances, I must think those States will be fond to be in confederacy with us. If we pay our quota of money annually, and furnish our ratable number of men, when necessary, I can see no danger from a rejection.

BAN ASSAULT BANANAS

DISTRICT OF COLUMBIA, ET AL., PETITIONERS v. DICK ANTHONY HELLER
on writ of certiorari to the united states court of appeals for the district of Columbia circuit

[June 26, 2008]

JUSTICE SCALIA delivered the opinion of the Court.

We consider whether a District of Columbia prohibition on the possession of usable handguns in the home violates the Second Amendment to the Constitution.

I

The District of Columbia generally prohibits the possession of handguns. It is a crime to carry an unregistered firearm, and the registration of handguns is prohibited. See D. C. Code §§7-2501.01(12), 7-2502.01(a), 7-2502.02(a)(4) (2001). Wholly apart from that prohibition, no person may carry a handgun without a license, but the chief of police may issue licenses for 1-year periods. See §§22-4504(a), 22-4506. District of Columbia law also requires residents to keep their lawfully owned firearms, such as registered long guns, "unloaded and dissembled or bound by a trigger lock or similar device" unless they are located in a place of business or are being used for lawful recreational activities. See §7-2507.02.1

Respondent Dick Heller is a D. C. special police officer authorized to carry a handgun while on duty at the Federal Judicial Center. He applied for a registration certificate for a handgun that he wished to keep at home, but the District refused. He thereafter filed a lawsuit in the Federal District Court for the District of Columbia seeking, on Second Amendment grounds, to enjoin the city from enforcing the bar on the registration of handguns, the licensing requirement insofar as it prohibits the carrying of a firearm in the home without a license, and the trigger-lock requirement insofar as it prohibits the use of "functional firearms within the home." App. 59a. The District Court dismissed respondent's complaint, see Parker v. District of Columbia, 311 F. Supp. 2d 103, 109 (2004). The Court of Appeals for the District of Columbia Circuit, construing his complaint as seeking the right to render a firearm operable and carry it about his home in that condition only when necessary for self-defense,2 reversed, see Parker v. District of Columbia, 478 F. 3d 370, 401 (2007). It held that the Second Amendment protects an individual right to possess firearms and that the city's total ban on handguns, as well as its requirement that firearms in the home be kept nonfunctional even when necessary for self-defense, violated that right. See id., at 395, 399-401. The Court of Appeals directed the District Court to enter summary judgment for respondent.

We granted certiorari. 552 U. S. ___ (2007).

II

We turn first to the meaning of the Second Amendment.

The Second Amendment provides: "A well regulated Militia, being necessary to the security of a free State, the right of the people to keep and bear Arms, shall not be infringed." In interpreting this text, we are guided by the principle that "[t]he Constitution was written to be understood by the voters; its words and phrases were used in their normal and ordinary as distinguished from technical meaning." United States v. Sprague, 282 U. S. 716, 731 (1931); see also Gibbons v. Ogden, 9 Wheat. 1, 188 (1824). Normal meaning may of course include an idiomatic meaning, but it excludes secret or technical meanings that would not have been known to ordinary citizens in the founding generation.

The two sides in this case have set out very different interpretations of the Amendment. Petitioners and today's dissenting Justices believe that it protects only the right to possess and carry a firearm in connection with militia service. See Brief for Petitioners 11-12; post, at 1 (STEVENS, J., dissenting). Respondent argues that it protects an individual right to possess a firearm unconnected with service in a militia, and to use that arm for traditionally lawful purposes, such as self-defense within the home. See Brief for Respondent 2-4.

The Second Amendment is naturally divided into two parts: its prefatory clause and its operative clause. The former does not limit the latter grammatically, but rather announces a purpose. The Amendment could be rephrased, "Because a well regulated Militia is necessary to the security of a free State, the right of the people to keep and bear Arms shall not be infringed." See J. Tiffany, A Treatise on Government and Constitutional Law §585, p. 394 (1867); Brief for Professors of Linguistics and English as Amici

Curiae 3 (hereinafter Linguists' Brief). Although this structure of the Second Amendment is unique in our Constitution, other legal documents of the founding era, particularly individual-rights provisions of state constitutions, commonly included a prefatory statement of purpose. See generally Volokh, The Commonplace Second Amendment, 73 N. Y. U. L. Rev. 793, 814-821 (1998).

Logic demands that there be a link between the stated purpose and the command. The Second Amendment would be nonsensical if it read, "A well regulated Militia, being necessary to the security of a free State, the right of the people to petition for redress of grievances shall not be infringed." That requirement of logical connection may cause a prefatory clause to resolve an ambiguity in the operative clause ("The separation of church and state being an important objective, the teachings of canons shall have no place in our jurisprudence." The preface makes clear that the operative clause refers not to canons of interpretation but to clergymen.) But apart from that clarifying function, a prefatory clause does not limit or expand the scope of the operative clause. See F. Dwarris, A General Treatise on Statutes 268-269 (P. Potter ed. 1871) (hereinafter Dwarris); T. Sedgwick, The Interpretation and Construction of Statutory and Constitutional Law 42-45 (2d ed. 1874).3 " 'It is nothing unusual in acts ... for the enacting part to go beyond the preamble; the remedy often extends beyond the particular act or mischief which first suggested the necessity of the law.' " J. Bishop, Commentaries on Written Laws and Their Interpretation §51, p. 49 (1882) (quoting Rex v. Marks, 3 East, 157, 165 (K. B. 1802)).

Therefore, while we will begin our textual analysis with the operative clause, we will return to the prefatory clause to ensure that our reading of the operative clause is consistent with the announced purpose.4

1. Operative Clause.

a. "Right of the People." The first salient feature of the operative clause is that it codifies a "right of the people." The unamended Constitution and the Bill of Rights use the phrase "right of the people" two other times, in the First Amendment's Assembly-and-Petition Clause and in the Fourth Amendment's Search-and-Seizure Clause. The Ninth Amendment uses very similar terminology ("The enumeration in the Constitution, of certain rights, shall not be construed to deny or disparage others retained by the people"). All three of these instances unambiguously refer to individual rights, not "collective" rights, or rights that may be exercised only through participation in some corporate body.5

Three provisions of the Constitution refer to "the people" in a context other than "rights"--the famous preamble ("We the people"), §2 of Article I (providing that "the people" will choose members of the House), and the Tenth Amendment (providing that those powers not given the Federal Government remain with "the States" or "the people"). Those provisions arguably refer to "the people" acting collectively--but they deal with the exercise or reservation of powers, not rights. Nowhere else in the

Constitution does a "right" attributed to "the people" refer to anything other than an individual right.6

What is more, in all six other provisions of the Constitution that mention "the people," the term unambiguously refers to all members of the political community, not an unspecified subset. As we said in United States v. Verdugo-Urquidez, 494 U. S. 259, 265 (1990):

"'[T]he people' seems to have been a term of art employed in select parts of the Constitution... . [Its uses] sugges[t] that 'the people' protected by the Fourth Amendment, and by the First and Second Amendments, and to whom rights and powers are reserved in the Ninth and Tenth Amendments, refers to a class of persons who are part of a national community or who have otherwise developed sufficient connection with this country to be considered part of that community."

This contrasts markedly with the phrase "the militia" in the prefatory clause. As we will describe below, the "militia" in colonial America consisted of a subset of "the people"--those who were male, able bodied, and within a certain age range. Reading the Second Amendment as protecting only the right to "keep and bear Arms" in an organized militia therefore fits poorly with the operative clause's description of the holder of that right as "the people."

BAN ASSAULT BANANAS

We start therefore with a strong presumption that the Second Amendment right is exercised individually and belongs to all Americans.

b. "Keep and bear Arms." We move now from the holder of the right--"the people"--to the substance of the right: "to keep and bear Arms."

Before addressing the verbs "keep" and "bear," we interpret their object: "Arms." The 18th-century meaning is no different from the meaning today. The 1773 edition of Samuel Johnson's dictionary defined "arms" as "weapons of offence, or armour of defence." 1 Dictionary of the English Language 107 (4th ed.) (hereinafter Johnson). Timothy Cunningham's important 1771 legal dictionary defined "arms" as "any thing that a man wears for his defence, or takes into his hands, or useth in wrath to cast at or strike another." 1 A New and Complete Law Dictionary (1771); see also N. Webster, American Dictionary of the English Language (1828) (reprinted 1989) (hereinafter Webster) (similar).

The term was applied, then as now, to weapons that were not specifically designed for military use and were not employed in a military capacity. For instance, Cunningham's legal dictionary gave as an example of usage: "Servants and labourers shall use bows and arrows on Sundays, &c. and not bear other arms." See also, e.g., An Act for the trial of Negroes, 1797 Del. Laws ch. XLIII, §6, p. 104, in 1 First Laws of the State of Delaware 102, 104 (J. Cushing ed. 1981 (pt. 1)); see generally State v. Duke, 42 Tex. 455, 458 (1874) (citing decisions of state courts construing "arms"). Although one founding-era thesaurus limited "arms" (as opposed to "weapons") to "instruments of offence generally made use of in war," even that source stated that all firearms constituted "arms." 1 J. Trusler, The Distinction Between Words Esteemed Synonymous in the English Language 37 (1794) (emphasis added).

Some have made the argument, bordering on the frivolous, that only those arms in existence in the 18th century are protected by the Second Amendment. We do not interpret constitutional rights that way. Just as the First Amendment protects modern forms of communications, e.g., Reno v. American Civil Liberties Union, 521 U. S. 844, 849 (1997), and the Fourth Amendment applies to modern forms of search, e.g., Kyllo v. United States, 533 U. S. 27, 35-36 (2001), the Second Amendment extends, prima facie, to all instruments that constitute bearable arms, even those that were not in existence at the time of the founding.

We turn to the phrases "keep arms" and "bear arms." Johnson defined "keep" as, most relevantly, "[t]o retain; not to lose," and "[t]o have in custody." Johnson 1095. Webster defined it as "[t]o hold; to retain in one's power or possession." No party has apprised us of an idiomatic meaning of "keep Arms." Thus, the most natural reading of "keep Arms" in the Second Amendment is to "have weapons."

The phrase "keep arms" was not prevalent in the written documents of the founding period that we have found, but there are a few examples, all of which favor viewing the right to "keep Arms" as an individual right unconnected with militia service. William Blackstone, for example, wrote that Catholics convicted of not attending service in the Church of England suffered certain penalties, one of which was that they were not permitted to "keep arms in their houses." 4 Commentaries on the Laws of England 55 (1769) (hereinafter Blackstone); see also 1 W. & M., c. 15, §4, in 3 Eng. Stat. at Large 422 (1689) ("[N]o Papist ... shall or may have or keep in his House ... any Arms ... "); 1 Hawkins, Treatise on the Pleas of the Crown 26 (1771) (similar). Petitioners point to militia laws of the founding period that required militia members to "keep" arms in connection with militia service, and they conclude from this that the phrase "keep Arms" has a militia-related connotation. See Brief for Petitioners 16-17 (citing laws of Delaware, New Jersey, and Virginia). This is rather like saying that, since there are many statutes that authorize aggrieved employees to "file complaints" with federal agencies, the phrase "file complaints" has an employment-related connotation. "Keep arms" was simply a common way of referring to possessing arms, for militiamen and everyone else.7

At the time of the founding, as now, to "bear" meant to "carry." See Johnson 161; Webster; T. Sheridan, A Complete Dictionary of the English Language (1796); 2 Oxford English Dictionary 20 (2d ed. 1989) (hereinafter Oxford). When used with "arms," however, the term has a meaning that refers to carrying for a particular purpose--confrontation. In Muscarello v. United States, 524 U. S. 125 (1998), in the course of analyzing the meaning of "carries a firearm" in a federal criminal statute, JUSTICE GINSBURG wrote that "[s]urely a most familiar meaning is, as the Constitution's Second Amendment ... indicate[s]: 'wear, bear, or carry ... upon the person or in the clothing or in a pocket, for the purpose ... of being armed and ready for offensive or defensive action in a case of conflict with another person.' " Id., at 143 (dissenting opinion) (quoting Black's Law Dictionary 214 (6th ed. 1998)). We think that JUSTICE GINSBURG accurately captured the natural meaning of "bear arms." Although the phrase implies that the carrying of the weapon is for the purpose of "offensive or defensive action," it in no way connotes participation in a structured military organization.

From our review of founding-era sources, we conclude that this natural meaning was also the meaning that "bear arms" had in the 18th century. In numerous instances, "bear arms" was unambiguously used to refer to the carrying of weapons outside of an organized militia. The most prominent examples are those most relevant to the Second Amendment: Nine state constitutional provisions written in the 18th century or the first two decades of the 19th, which enshrined a right of citizens to "bear arms in defense of themselves and the state" or "bear arms in defense of himself and the state." 8 It is clear from those formulations that "bear arms" did not refer only to carrying a weapon in an organized military unit. Justice James Wilson interpreted the Pennsylvania Constitution's arms-bearing right, for example, as a recognition of the natural right of defense "of one's person or house"--what he called the law of "self preservation." 2 Collected Works of James Wilson 1142, and n. x (K. Hall & M. Hall eds. 2007) (citing Pa. Const., Art. IX, §21 (1790)); see also T. Walker, Introduction to American Law 198 (1837) ("Thus the right of self-defence [is] guaranteed by the [Ohio] constitution"); see also id., at 157 (equating Second Amendment with that provision of the Ohio Constitution). That was also the interpretation of those state constitutional provisions adopted by pre-Civil War state courts.9 These provisions demonstrate--again, in the most analogous linguistic context--that "bear arms" was not limited to the carrying of arms in a militia.

The phrase "bear Arms" also had at the time of the founding an idiomatic meaning that was significantly different from its natural meaning: "to serve as a soldier, do military service, fight" or "to wage war." See Linguists' Brief 18; post, at 11 (STEVENS, J., dissenting). But it unequivocally bore that idiomatic meaning only when followed by the preposition "against," which was in turn followed by the target of the hostilities. See 2 Oxford 21. (That is how, for example, our Declaration of Independence ¶28, used the phrase: "He has constrained our fellow Citizens taken Captive on the high Seas to bear Arms against their Country ... .") Every example given by petitioners' amici for the idiomatic meaning of "bear arms" from the founding period either includes the preposition "against" or is not clearly idiomatic. See Linguists' Brief 18-23. Without the preposition, "bear arms" normally meant (as it continues to mean today) what JUSTICE GINSBURG's opinion in Muscarello said.

In any event, the meaning of "bear arms" that petitioners and JUSTICE STEVENS propose is not even the (sometimes) idiomatic meaning. Rather, they manufacture a hybrid definition, whereby "bear arms" connotes the actual carrying of arms (and therefore is not really an idiom) but only in the service of an organized militia. No dictionary has ever adopted that definition, and we have been apprised of no source that indicates that it carried that meaning at the time of the founding. But it is easy to see why petitioners and the dissent are driven to the hybrid definition. Giving "bear Arms" its idiomatic meaning would cause the protected right to consist of the right to be a soldier or to wage war--an absurdity that no commentator has ever endorsed. See L. Levy, Origins of the Bill of Rights 135 (1999). Worse still, the phrase "keep and bear Arms" would be incoherent. The word "Arms" would have two different meanings at once: "weapons" (as the object of "keep") and (as the object of "bear") one-half of an idiom. It would be rather like saying "He filled and kicked the bucket" to mean "He filled the bucket and died." Grotesque.

Petitioners justify their limitation of "bear arms" to the military context by pointing out the unremarkable fact that it was often used in that context--the same mistake they made with respect to "keep arms." It is especially unremarkable that the phrase was often used in a military context in the federal legal sources (such as records of congressional debate) that have been the focus of petitioners' inquiry. Those sources would have had little occasion to use it except in discussions about the standing army and the militia. And the phrases used primarily in those military discussions include not only "bear arms" but also "carry arms," "possess arms," and "have arms"--though no one thinks that those other phrases also had special military meanings. See Barnett, Was the Right to Keep and Bear Arms Conditioned on Service in an Organized Militia?, 83 Tex. L. Rev. 237, 261 (2004). The common references to those "fit to bear arms" in congressional discussions about the militia are matched by use of the same phrase in the few nonmilitary federal contexts where the concept would be relevant. See, e.g., 30 Journals of Continental Congress 349-351 (J. Fitzpatrick ed. 1934). Other legal sources frequently used "bear arms" in nonmilitary contexts.10 Cunningham's legal dictionary, cited above, gave as an example of its usage a sentence unrelated to military affairs ("Servants and labourers shall use bows and arrows on Sundays, &c. and not bear other arms"). And if one looks beyond legal sources, "bear arms" was frequently used in nonmilitary contexts. See Cramer & Olson, What Did "Bear Arms" Mean in the Second Amendment?, 6 Georgetown J. L. & Pub. Pol'y (forthcoming Sept. 2008), online at http://papers.ssrn.com/abstract=1086176 (as visited June 24, 2008, and available in Clerk of Court's case file) (identifying numerous nonmilitary uses of "bear arms" from the founding period).

JUSTICE STEVENS points to a study by amici supposedly showing that the phrase "bear arms" was most frequently used in the military context. See post, at 12-13, n. 9; Linguists' Brief 24. Of course, as we have said, the fact that the phrase was commonly used in a particular context does not show that it is limited to that context, and, in any event, we have given many sources where the phrase was used in nonmilitary contexts. Moreover, the study's collection appears to include (who knows how many times) the idiomatic phrase "bear arms against," which is irrelevant. The amici also dismiss examples such as " 'bear arms ... for the purpose of killing game' " because those uses are "expressly qualified." Linguists' Brief 24. (JUSTICE STEVENS uses the same excuse for dismissing the state constitutional provisions analogous to the Second Amendment that identify private-use purposes for which the individual right can be asserted. See post, at 12.) That analysis is faulty. A purposive qualifying phrase that contradicts the word or phrase it modifies is unknown this side of the looking glass (except, apparently, in some courses on Linguistics). If "bear arms" means, as we think, simply the carrying of arms, a modifier can limit the purpose of the carriage ("for the purpose of self-defense" or "to make war against the King"). But if "bear arms" means, as the petitioners and the dissent think, the carrying of arms only for military purposes, one simply cannot add "for the purpose of killing game." The right "to carry arms in the militia for the purpose of killing game" is worthy of the mad hatter. Thus, these purposive qualifying phrases positively establish that "to bear arms" is not limited to military use.11

JUSTICE STEVENS places great weight on James Madison's inclusion of a conscientious-objector clause in his original draft of the Second Amendment: "but no person religiously scrupulous of bearing arms, shall be compelled to render military service in person." Creating the Bill of

Rights 12 (H. Veit, K. Bowling, & C. Bickford eds. 1991) (hereinafter Veit). He argues that this clause establishes that the drafters of the Second Amendment intended "bear Arms" to refer only to military service. See post, at 26. It is always perilous to derive the meaning of an adopted provision from another provision deleted in the drafting process.12 In any case, what JUSTICE STEVENS would conclude from the deleted provision does not follow. It was not meant to exempt from military service those who objected to going to war but had no scruples about personal gunfights. Quakers opposed the use of arms not just for militia service, but for any violent purpose whatsoever--so much so that Quaker frontiersmen were forbidden to use arms to defend their families, even though "[i]n such circumstances the temptation to seize a hunting rifle or knife in self-defense ... must sometimes have been almost overwhelming." P. Brock, Pacifism in the United States 359 (1968); see M. Hirst, The Quakers in Peace and War 336-339 (1923); 3 T. Clarkson, Portraiture of Quakerism 103-104 (3d ed. 1807). The Pennsylvania Militia Act of 1757 exempted from service those "scrupling the use of arms"--a phrase that no one contends had an idiomatic meaning. See 5 Stat. at Large of Pa. 613 (J. Mitchell & H. Flanders eds. 1898) (emphasis added). Thus, the most natural interpretation of Madison's deleted text is that those opposed to carrying weapons for potential violent confrontation would not be "compelled to render military service," in which such carrying would be required.13

Finally, JUSTICE STEVENS suggests that "keep and bear Arms" was some sort of term of art, presumably akin to "hue and cry" or "cease and desist." (This suggestion usefully evades the problem that there is no evidence whatsoever to support a military reading of "keep arms.") JUSTICE STEVENS believes that the unitary meaning of "keep and bear Arms" is established by the Second Amendment's calling it a "right" (singular) rather than "rights" (plural). See post, at 16. There is nothing to this. State constitutions of the founding period routinely grouped multiple (related) guarantees under a singular "right," and the First Amendment protects the "right [singular] of the people peaceably to assemble, and to petition the Government for a redress of grievances." See, e.g., Pa. Declaration of Rights §§IX, XII, XVI, in 5 Thorpe 3083-3084; Ohio Const., Arts. VIII, §§11, 19 (1802), in id., at 2910-2911.14 And even if "keep and bear Arms" were a unitary phrase, we find no evidence that it bore a military meaning. Although the phrase was not at all common (which would be unusual for a term of art), we have found instances of its use with a clearly nonmilitary connotation. In a 1780 debate in the House of Lords, for example, Lord Richmond described an order to disarm private citizens (not militia members) as "a violation of the constitutional right of Protestant subjects to keep and bear arms for their own defense." 49 The London Magazine or Gentleman's Monthly Intelligencer 467 (1780). In response, another member of Parliament referred to "the right of bearing arms for personal defence," making clear that no special military meaning for "keep and bear arms" was intended in the discussion. Id., at 467-468.15

c. Meaning of the Operative Clause. Putting all of these textual elements together, we find that they guarantee the individual right to possess and carry weapons in case of confrontation. This meaning is strongly confirmed by the historical background of the Second Amendment. We look to this because it has always been widely understood that the Second Amendment, like the First and Fourth Amendments, codified a pre-existing right. The very text of the Second Amendment implicitly recognizes the pre-existence of the right and declares only that it "shall not be infringed." As we said in United States v. Cruikshank, 92 U. S. 542, 553 (1876), "[t]his is not a right granted by the Constitution. Neither is it in any manner dependent upon that instrument for its existence. The Second amendment declares that it shall not be infringed ... ."16

Between the Restoration and the Glorious Revolution, the Stuart Kings Charles II and James II succeeded in using select militias loyal to them to suppress political dissidents, in part by disarming their opponents. See J. Malcolm, To Keep and Bear Arms 31-53 (1994) (hereinafter Malcolm); L. Schwoerer, The Declaration of Rights, 1689, p. 76 (1981). Under the auspices of the 1671 Game Act, for example, the Catholic James II had ordered general disarmaments of regions home to his Protestant enemies. See Malcolm 103-106. These experiences caused Englishmen to be extremely wary of concentrated military forces run by the state and to be jealous of their arms. They accordingly obtained an assurance from William and Mary, in the Declaration of Right (which was codified as the English Bill of Rights), that Protestants would never be disarmed: "That the subjects which are Protestants may have arms for their defense suitable to their conditions and as allowed by law." 1 W. & M., c. 2, §7, in 3 Eng. Stat. at Large 441 (1689). This right has long been understood to be the predecessor to our Second Amendment. See E. Dumbauld, The Bill of Rights and What It Means Today 51 (1957); W. Rawle, A View of the Constitution of the United States of America 122 (1825) (hereinafter Rawle). It was clearly an individual right, having nothing whatever to do with service in a militia. To be sure, it was an individual right not available to the whole population, given that it was restricted to Protestants, and like all written English rights it was held only against the Crown, not Parliament. See Schwoerer, To Hold and Bear Arms: The English Perspective, in Bogus 207, 218; but see 3 J. Story, Commentaries on the Constitution of the United States §1858 (1833) (hereinafter Story) (contending that the "right to bear arms" is a "limitatio[n] upon the power of parliament" as well). But it was secured to them as individuals, according to "libertarian political principles," not as members of a fighting force. Schwoerer, Declaration of Rights, at 283; see also id., at 78; G. Jellinek, The Declaration of the Rights of Man and of Citizens 49, and n. 7 (1901) (reprinted 1979).

By the time of the founding, the right to have arms had become fundamental for English subjects. See Malcolm 122-134. Blackstone, whose works, we have said, "constituted the preeminent authority on English law for the founding generation," Alden v. Maine, 527 U. S. 706, 715 (1999), cited the arms provision of the Bill of Rights as one of the fundamental rights of Englishmen. See 1

Blackstone 136, 139-140 (1765). His description of it cannot possibly be thought to tie it to militia or military service. It was, he said, "the natural right of resistance and self-preservation," id., at 139, and "the right of having and using arms for self-preservation and defence," id., at 140; see also 3 id., at 2-4 (1768). Other contemporary authorities concurred. See G. Sharp, Tracts, Concerning the Ancient and Only True Legal Means of National Defence, by a Free Militia 17-18, 27 (3d ed. 1782); 2 J. de Lolme, The Rise and Progress of the English Constitution 886-887 (1784) (A. Stephens ed. 1838); W. Blizard, Desultory Reflections on Police 59-60 (1785). Thus, the right secured in 1689 as a result of the Stuarts' abuses was by the time of the founding understood to be an individual right protecting against both public and private violence.

And, of course, what the Stuarts had tried to do to their political enemies, George III had tried to do to the colonists. In the tumultuous decades of the 1760's and 1770's, the Crown began to disarm the inhabitants of the most rebellious areas. That provoked polemical reactions by Americans invoking their rights as Englishmen to keep arms. A New York article of April 1769 said that "[i]t is a natural right which the people have reserved to themselves, confirmed by the Bill of Rights, to keep arms for their own defence." A Journal of the Times: Mar. 17, New York Journal, Supp. 1, Apr. 13, 1769, in Boston Under Military Rule 79 (O. Dickerson ed. 1936); see also, e.g., Shippen, Boston Gazette, Jan. 30, 1769, in 1 The Writings of Samuel Adams 299 (H. Cushing ed. 1968). They understood the right to enable individuals to defend themselves. As the most important early American edition of Blackstone's Commentaries (by the law professor and former Antifederalist St. George Tucker) made clear in the notes to the description of the arms right, Americans understood the "right of self-preservation" as permitting a citizen to "repe[l] force by force" when "the intervention of society in his behalf, may be too late to prevent an injury." 1 Blackstone's Commentaries 145-146, n. 42 (1803) (hereinafter Tucker's Blackstone). See also W. Duer, Outlines of the Constitutional Jurisprudence of the United States 31-32 (1833).

There seems to us no doubt, on the basis of both text and history, that the Second Amendment conferred an individual right to keep and bear arms. Of course the right was not unlimited, just as the First Amendment's right of free speech was not, see, e.g., United States v. Williams, 553 U. S. ___ (2008). Thus, we do not read the Second Amendment to protect the right of citizens to carry arms for any sort of confrontation, just as we do not read the First Amendment to protect the right of citizens to speak for any purpose. Before turning to limitations upon the individual right, however, we must determine whether the prefatory clause of the Second Amendment comports with our interpretation of the operative clause.

2. Prefatory Clause.

The prefatory clause reads: "A well regulated Militia, being necessary to the security of a free State ... ."

a. "Well-Regulated Militia." In United States v. Miller, 307 U. S. 174, 179 (1939), we explained that "the Militia comprised all males physically capable of acting in concert for the common defense." That definition comports with founding-era sources. See, e.g., Webster ("The militia of a country are the able bodied men organized into companies, regiments and brigades ... and required by law to attend military exercises on certain days only, but at other times left to pursue their usual occupations"); The Federalist No. 46, pp. 329, 334 (B. Wright ed. 1961) (J. Madison) ("near half a million of citizens with arms in their hands"); Letter to Destutt de Tracy (Jan. 26, 1811), in The Portable Thomas Jefferson 520, 524 (M. Peterson ed. 1975) ("[T]he militia of the State, that is to say, of every man in it able to bear arms").

Petitioners take a seemingly narrower view of the militia, stating that "[m]ilitias are the state- and congressionally-regulated military forces described in the Militia Clauses (art. I, §8, cls. 15-16)." Brief for Petitioners 12. Although we agree with petitioners' interpretive assumption that "militia" means the same thing in Article I and the Second Amendment, we believe that petitioners identify the wrong thing, namely, the organized militia. Unlike armies and navies, which Congress is given the power to create ("to raise ... Armies"; "to provide ... a Navy," Art. I, §8, cls. 12-13), the militia is assumed by Article I already to be in existence. Congress is given the power to "provide for calling forth the militia," §8, cl. 15; and the power not to create, but to "organiz[e]" it--and not to organize "a" militia, which is what one would expect if the militia were to be a federal creation, but to organize "the" militia, connoting a body already in existence, ibid., cl. 16. This is fully consistent with the ordinary definition of the militia as all able-bodied men. From that pool, Congress has plenary power to organize the units that will make up an effective fighting force. That is what Congress did in the first militia Act, which specified that "each and every free able-bodied white male citizen of the respective states, resident therein, who is or shall be of the age of eighteen years, and under the age of forty-five years (except as is herein after excepted) shall severally and respectively be enrolled in the militia." Act of May 8, 1792, 1 Stat. 271. To be sure, Congress need not conscript every able-bodied man into the militia, because nothing in Article I suggests that in exercising its power to organize, discipline, and arm the militia, Congress must focus upon the entire body. Although the militia consists of all able-bodied men, the federally organized militia may consist of a subset of them.

Finally, the adjective "well-regulated" implies nothing more than the imposition of proper discipline and training. See Johnson 1619 ("Regulate": "To adjust by rule or method"); Rawle 121-122; cf. Va. Declaration of Rights §13 (1776), in 7 Thorpe 3812, 3814 (referring to "a well-regulated militia, composed of the body of the people, trained to arms").

b. "Security of a Free State." The phrase "security of a free state" meant "security of a free polity," not security of each of the several States as the dissent below argued, see 478 F. 3d, at 405, and n. 10. Joseph Story wrote in his treatise on the Constitution that "the word 'state' is used in various senses [and in] its most enlarged sense, it means the people composing a particular nation or community." 1 Story §208; see also 3 id., §1890 (in reference to the Second Amendment's prefatory clause: "The militia is the natural defence of a free country"). It is true that the term "State" elsewhere in the Constitution refers to individual States, but the phrase "security of a free state" and close variations seem to have been terms of art in 18th-century political discourse, meaning a " 'free country' " or free polity. See Volokh, "Necessary to the Security of a Free State," 83 Notre Dame L. Rev. 1, 5 (2007); see, e.g., 4 Blackstone 151 (1769); Brutus Essay III (Nov. 15, 1787), in The Essential Antifederalist 251, 253 (W. Allen & G. Lloyd eds., 2d ed. 2002). Moreover, the other instances of "state" in the Constitution are typically accompanied by modifiers making clear that the reference is to the several States--"each state," "several states," "any state," "that state," "particular states," "one state," "no state." And the presence of the term "foreign state" in Article I and Article III shows that the word "state" did not have a single meaning in the Constitution.

There are many reasons why the militia was thought to be "necessary to the security of a free state." See 3 Story §1890. First, of course, it is useful in repelling invasions and suppressing insurrections. Second, it renders large standing armies unnecessary--an argument that Alexander Hamilton made in favor of federal control over the militia. The Federalist No. 29, pp. 226, 227 (B. Wright ed. 1961) (A. Hamilton). Third, when the able-bodied men of a nation are trained in arms and organized, they are better able to resist tyranny.

3. Relationship between Prefatory Clause and Operative Clause

We reach the question, then: Does the preface fit with an operative clause that creates an individual right to keep and bear arms? It fits perfectly, once one knows the history that the founding generation knew and that we have described above. That history showed that the way tyrants had eliminated a militia consisting of all the able-bodied men was not by banning the militia but simply by taking away the people's arms, enabling a select militia or standing army to suppress political opponents. This is what had occurred in England that prompted codification of the right to have arms in the English Bill of Rights.

The debate with respect to the right to keep and bear arms, as with other guarantees in the Bill of Rights, was not over whether it was desirable (all agreed that it was) but over whether it needed to be codified in the Constitution. During the 1788 ratification debates, the fear that the federal government would disarm the people in order to impose rule through a standing army or select militia was pervasive in Antifederalist rhetoric. See, e.g., Letters from The Federal Farmer III (Oct. 10, 1787), in 2 The Complete Anti-Federalist 234, 242 (H. Storing ed. 1981). John Smilie, for example, worried not only that Congress's "command of the militia" could be used to create a "select militia," or to have "no militia at all," but also, as a separate concern, that "[w]hen a select militia is formed; the people in general may be disarmed." 2 Documentary History of the Ratification of the Constitution 508-509 (M. Jensen ed. 1976) (hereinafter Documentary Hist.). Federalists responded that because Congress was given no power to abridge the ancient right of individuals to keep and bear arms, such a force could never oppress the people. See, e.g., A Pennsylvanian III (Feb. 20, 1788), in The Origin of the Second Amendment 275, 276 (D. Young ed., 2d ed. 2001) (hereinafter Young); White, To the Citizens of Virginia, Feb. 22, 1788, in id., at 280, 281; A Citizen of America, (Oct. 10, 1787) in id., at 38, 40; Remarks on the Amendments to the federal Constitution, Nov. 7, 1788, in id., at 556. It was understood across the political spectrum that the right helped to secure the ideal of a citizen militia, which might be necessary to oppose an oppressive military force if the constitutional order broke down.

It is therefore entirely sensible that the Second Amendment's prefatory clause announces the purpose for which the right was codified: to prevent elimination of the militia. The prefatory clause does not suggest that preserving the militia was the only reason Americans valued the ancient right; most undoubtedly thought it even more important for self-defense and hunting. But the threat that the new Federal Government would destroy the citizens' militia by taking away their arms was the reason that right--unlike some other English rights--was codified in a written Constitution. JUSTICE BREYER's assertion that individual self-defense is merely a "subsidiary interest" of the right to keep and bear arms, see post, at 36, is profoundly mistaken. He bases that assertion solely upon the prologue--but that can only show that self-defense had little to do with the right's codification; it was the central component of the right itself.

Besides ignoring the historical reality that the Second Amendment was not intended to lay down a "novel principl[e]" but rather codified a right "inherited from our English ancestors," Robertson v. Baldwin, 165 U. S. 275, 281 (1897), petitioners' interpretation does not even achieve the narrower purpose that prompted codification of the right. If, as they believe, the Second Amendment right is no more than the right to keep and use weapons as a member of an organized militia, see Brief for Petitioners 8--if, that is, the organized militia is the sole institutional beneficiary of the Second Amendment's guarantee--it does not assure the existence of a "citizens' militia" as a safeguard against tyranny. For Congress retains plenary authority to organize the militia, which must include the authority to say who will belong to the organized force.17 That is why the first Militia Act's requirement that only whites enroll caused States to amend their militia laws to exclude free blacks. See Siegel, The Federal Government's Power to Enact Color-Conscious Laws, 92 Nw. U. L. Rev. 477, 521-525 (1998). Thus, if petitioners are correct, the Second Amendment protects citizens' right to use a gun in an organization from which Congress has plenary authority to exclude them. It guarantees a select militia of the sort the Stuart kings found useful, but not the people's militia that was the concern of the founding generation.

BAN ASSAULT BANANAS

B

Our interpretation is confirmed by analogous arms-bearing rights in state constitutions that preceded and immediately followed adoption of the Second Amendment. Four States adopted analogues to the Federal Second Amendment in the period between independence and the ratification of the Bill of Rights. Two of them--Pennsylvania and Vermont--clearly adopted individual rights unconnected to militia service. Pennsylvania's Declaration of Rights of 1776 said: "That the people have a right to bear arms for the defence of themselves, and the state ... ." §XIII, in 5 Thorpe 3082, 3083 (emphasis added). In 1777, Vermont adopted the identical provision, except for inconsequential differences in punctuation and capitalization. See Vt. Const., ch. 1, §15, in 6 id., at 3741.

North Carolina also codified a right to bear arms in 1776: "That the people have a right to bear arms, for the defence of the State ... ." Declaration of Rights §XVII, in id., at 2787, 2788. This could plausibly be read to support only a right to bear arms in a militia--but that is a peculiar way to make the point in a constitution that elsewhere repeatedly mentions the militia explicitly. See §§14, 18, 35, in 5 id., 2789, 2791, 2793. Many colonial statutes required individual arms-bearing for public-safety reasons--such as the 1770 Georgia law that "for the security and defence of this province from internal dangers and insurrections" required those men who qualified for militia duty individually "to carry fire arms" "to places of public worship." 19 Colonial Records of the State of Georgia

137-139 (A. Candler ed. 1911 (pt. 2)) (emphasis added). That broad public-safety understanding was the connotation given to the North Carolina right by that State's Supreme Court in 1843. See State v. Huntly, 3 Ired. 418, 422-423.

The 1780 Massachusetts Constitution presented another variation on the theme: "The people have a right to keep and to bear arms for the common defence... ." Pt. First, Art. XVII, in 3 Thorpe 1888, 1892. Once again, if one gives narrow meaning to the phrase "common defence" this can be thought to limit the right to the bearing of arms in a state-organized military force. But once again the State's highest court thought otherwise. Writing for the court in an 1825 libel case, Chief Justice Parker wrote: "The liberty of the press was to be unrestrained, but he who used it was to be responsible in cases of its abuse; like the right to keep fire arms, which does not protect him who uses them for annoyance or destruction." Commonwealth v. Blanding, 20 Mass. 304, 313-314. The analogy makes no sense if firearms could not be used for any individual purpose at all. See also Kates, Handgun Prohibition and the Original Meaning of the Second Amendment, 82 Mich. L. Rev. 204, 244 (1983) (19th-century courts never read "common defence" to limit the use of weapons to militia service).

We therefore believe that the most likely reading of all four of these pre-Second Amendment state constitutional provisions is that they secured an individual right to bear arms for defensive purposes. Other States did not include rights to bear arms in their pre-1789 constitutions--although in Virginia a Second Amendment analogue was proposed (unsuccessfully) by Thomas Jefferson. (It read: "No freeman shall ever be debarred the use of arms [within his own lands or tenements]."18 1 The Papers of Thomas Jefferson 344 (J. Boyd ed. 1950)).

Between 1789 and 1820, nine States adopted Second Amendment analogues. Four of them--Kentucky, Ohio, Indiana, and Missouri--referred to the right of the people to "bear arms in defence of themselves and the State." See n. 8, supra. Another three States--Mississippi, Connecticut, and Alabama--used the even more individualistic phrasing that each citizen has the "right to bear arms in defence of himself and the State." See ibid. Finally, two States--Tennessee and Maine--used the "common defence" language of Massachusetts. See Tenn. Const., Art. XI, §26 (1796), in 6 Thorpe 3414, 3424; Me. Const., Art. I, §16 (1819), in 3 id., at 1646, 1648. That of the nine state constitutional protections for the right to bear arms enacted immediately after 1789 at least seven unequivocally protected an individual citizen's right to self-defense is strong evidence that that is how the founding generation conceived of the right. And with one possible exception that we discuss in Part II-D-2, 19th-century courts and commentators interpreted these state constitutional provisions to protect an individual right to use arms for self-defense. See n. 9, supra; Simpson v. State, 5 Yer. 356, 360 (Tenn. 1833).

The historical narrative that petitioners must endorse would thus treat the Federal Second Amendment as an odd outlier, protecting a right unknown in state constitutions or at English common law, based on little more than an overreading of the prefatory clause.

C

JUSTICE STEVENS relies on the drafting history of the Second Amendment--the various proposals in the state conventions and the debates in Congress. It is dubious to rely on such history to interpret a text that was widely understood to codify a pre-existing right, rather than to fashion a new one. But even assuming that this legislative history is relevant, JUSTICE STEVENS flatly misreads the historical record.

It is true, as JUSTICE STEVENS says, that there was concern that the Federal Government would abolish the institution of the state militia. See post, at 20. That concern found expression, however, not in the various Second Amendment precursors proposed in the State conventions, but in separate structural provisions that would have given the States concurrent and seemingly nonpre-emptible authority to organize, discipline, and arm the militia when the Federal Government failed to do so. See Veit 17, 20 (Virginia proposal); 4 J. Eliot, The Debates in the Several State Conventions on the Adoption of the Federal Constitution 244, 245 (2d ed. 1836) (reprinted 1941) (North Carolina proposal); see also 2 Documentary Hist. 624 (Pennsylvania minority's proposal). The Second

Amendment precursors, by contrast, referred to the individual English right already codified in two (and probably four) State constitutions. The Federalist-dominated first Congress chose to reject virtually all major structural revisions favored by the Antifederalists, including the proposed militia amendments. Rather, it adopted primarily the popular and uncontroversial (though, in the Federalists' view, unnecessary) individual-rights amendments. The Second Amendment right, protecting only individuals' liberty to keep and carry arms, did nothing to assuage Antifederalists' concerns about federal control of the militia. See, e.g., Centinel, Revived, No. XXIX, Philadelphia Independent Gazetteer, Sept. 9, 1789, in Young 711, 712.

JUSTICE STEVENS thinks it significant that the Virginia, New York, and North Carolina Second Amendment proposals were "embedded ... within a group of principles that are distinctly military in meaning," such as statements about the danger of standing armies. Post, at 22. But so was the highly influential minority proposal in Pennsylvania, yet that proposal, with its reference to hunting, plainly referred to an individual right. See 2 Documentary Hist. 624. Other than that erroneous point, JUSTICE STEVENS has brought forward absolutely no evidence that those proposals conferred only a right to carry arms in a militia. By contrast, New Hampshire's proposal, the Pennsylvania minority's proposal, and Samuel Adams' proposal in Massachusetts unequivocally referred to individual rights, as did two state constitutional provisions at the time. See Veit 16, 17 (New Hampshire proposal); 6 Documentary Hist. 1452, 1453 (J.

Kaminski & G. Saladino eds. 2000) (Samuel Adams' proposal). JUSTICE STEVENS' view thus relies on the proposition, unsupported by any evidence, that different people of the founding period had vastly different conceptions of the right to keep and bear arms. That simply does not comport with our longstanding view that the Bill of Rights codified venerable, widely understood liberties.

D

We now address how the Second Amendment was interpreted from immediately after its ratification through the end of the 19th century. Before proceeding, however, we take issue with JUSTICE STEVENS' equating of these sources with postenactment legislative history, a comparison that betrays a fundamental misunderstanding of a court's interpretive task. See post, at 27, n. 28. "Legislative history," of course, refers to the pre-enactment statements of those who drafted or voted for a law; it is considered persuasive by some, not because they reflect the general understanding of the disputed terms, but because the legislators who heard or read those statements presumably voted with that understanding. Ibid. "Postenactment legislative history," ibid., a deprecatory contradiction in terms, refers to statements of those who drafted or voted for the law that are made after its enactment and hence could have had no effect on the congressional vote. It most certainly does not refer to the examination of a variety of legal and other sources to determine the public understanding of a legal text in the period after its enactment or ratification. That sort of inquiry is a critical tool of constitutional interpretation. As we will show, virtually all interpreters of the Second Amendment in the century after its enactment interpreted the amendment as we do.

1. Post-ratification Commentary

Three important founding-era legal scholars interpreted the Second Amendment in published writings. All three understood it to protect an individual right unconnected with militia service.

St. George Tucker's version of Blackstone's Commentaries, as we explained above, conceived of the Blackstonian arms right as necessary for self-defense. He equated that right, absent the religious and class-based restrictions, with the Second Amendment. See 2 Tucker's Blackstone 143. In Note D, entitled, "View of the Constitution of the United States," Tucker elaborated on the Second Amendment: "This may be considered as the true palladium of liberty .... The right to self-defence is the first law of nature: in most governments it has been the study of rulers to confine the right within the narrowest limits possible. Wherever standing armies are kept up, and the right of the people to keep and bear arms is, under any colour or pretext whatsoever, prohibited, liberty, if not already annihilated, is on the brink of destruction." 1 id., at App. 300 (ellipsis in original). He believed that the English game laws had abridged the right by prohibiting "keeping a gun or other engine for the destruction of game." Ibid; see also 2 id., at 143, and nn. 40 and 41. He later grouped the right with some of the individual rights included in the First Amendment and said that if "a law be passed by congress, prohibiting" any of those rights, it would "be the province of the judiciary to pronounce whether any such act were constitutional, or not; and if not, to acquit the accused ... ." 1 id., at App. 357. It is unlikely that Tucker was referring to a person's being "accused" of violating a law making it a crime to bear arms in a state militia.

In 1825, William Rawle, a prominent lawyer who had been a member of the Pennsylvania Assembly that ratified the Bill of Rights, published an influential treatise, which analyzed the Second Amendment as follows:

"The first [principle] is a declaration that a well regulated militia is necessary to the security of a free state; a proposition from which few will dissent... .

"The corollary, from the first position is, that the right of the people to keep and bear arms shall not be infringed.

"The prohibition is general. No clause in the constitution could by any rule of construction be conceived to give to congress a power to disarm the people. Such a flagitious attempt could only be made under some general pretence by a state legislature. But if in any blind pursuit of inordinate power, either should attempt it, this amendment may be appealed to as a restraint on both." Rawle 121-122.20

Like Tucker, Rawle regarded the English game laws as violating the right codified in the Second Amendment. See id., 122-123. Rawle clearly differentiated between the people's right to bear arms and their service in a militia: "In a people permitted and accustomed to bear arms, we have the rudiments of a militia, which properly consists of armed citizens, divided into military bands, and instructed at least in part, in the use of arms for the purposes of war." Id., at 140. Rawle further said that the Second Amendment right ought not "be abused to the disturbance of the public peace," such as by assembling with other armed individuals "for an unlawful purpose"--statements that make no sense if the right does not extend to any individual purpose.

Joseph Story published his famous Commentaries on the Constitution of the United States in 1833. JUSTICE STEVENS suggests that "[t]here is not so much as a whisper" in Story's explanation of the Second Amendment that favors the individual-rights view. Post, at 34. That is wrong. Story explained that the English Bill of Rights had also included a "right to bear arms," a right that, as we have discussed, had nothing to do with militia service. 3 Story §1858. He then equated the English right with the Second Amendment:

"§1891. A similar provision [to the Second Amendment] in favour of protestants (for to them it is confined) is to be found in the bill of rights of 1688, it being declared, 'that the subjects, which are protestants, may have arms for their defence suitable to their condition, and as allowed by law.' But under various pretences the effect of this provision has been greatly narrowed; and it is at present in England more nominal than real, as a defensive privilege." (Footnotes omitted.)

This comparison to the Declaration of Right would not make sense if the Second Amendment right was the right to use a gun in a militia, which was plainly not what the English right protected. As the Tennessee Supreme Court recognized 38 years after Story wrote his Commentaries, "[t]he passage from Story, shows clearly that this right was intended ... and was guaranteed to, and to be exercised and enjoyed by the citizen as such, and not by him as a soldier, or in defense solely of his political rights." Andrews v. State, 50 Tenn. 165, 183 (1871). Story's Commentaries also cite as support Tucker and Rawle, both of whom clearly viewed the right as unconnected to militia service. See 3 Story §1890, n. 2; §1891, n. 3. In addition, in a shorter 1840 work Story wrote: "One of the ordinary modes, by which tyrants accomplish their purposes without resistance, is, by disarming the people, and making it an offence to keep arms, and by substituting a regular army in the stead of a resort to the militia." A Familiar Exposition of the Constitution of the United States §450 (reprinted in 1986).

Antislavery advocates routinely invoked the right to bear arms for self-defense. Joel Tiffany, for example, citing Blackstone's description of the right, wrote that "the right to keep and bear arms, also implies the right to use them if necessary in self defence; without this right to use the guaranty would have hardly been worth the paper it consumed." A Treatise on the Unconstitutionality of

American Slavery 117-118 (1849); see also L. Spooner, The Unconstitutionality of Slavery 116 (1845) (right enables "personal defence"). In his famous Senate speech about the 1856 "Bleeding Kansas" conflict, Charles Sumner proclaimed:

"The rifle has ever been the companion of the pioneer and, under God, his tutelary protector against the red man and the beast of the forest. Never was this efficient weapon more needed in just self-defence, than now in Kansas, and at least one article in our National Constitution must be blotted out, before the complete right to it can in any way be impeached. And yet such is the madness of the hour, that, in defiance of the solemn guarantee, embodied in the Amendments to the Constitution, that 'the right of the people to keep and bear arms shall not be infringed,' the people of Kansas have been arraigned for keeping and bearing them, and the Senator from South Carolina has had the face to say openly, on this floor, that they should be disarmed--of course, that the fanatics of Slavery, his allies and constituents, may meet no impediment." The Crime Against Kansas, May 19-20, 1856, in American Speeches: Political Oratory from the Revolution to the Civil War 553, 606-607 (2006).

We have found only one early 19th-century commentator who clearly conditioned the right to keep and bear arms upon service in the militia--and he recognized that the prevailing view was to the contrary. "The provision of the constitution, declaring the right of the people to keep and bear arms, &c. was probably intended to apply to the right of the people to bear arms for such [militia-related] purposes only, and not to prevent congress or the legislatures of the different states from enacting laws to prevent the citizens from always going armed. A different construction however has been given to it." B. Oliver, The Rights of an American Citizen 177 (1832).

2. Pre-Civil War Case Law

The 19th-century cases that interpreted the Second Amendment universally support an individual right unconnected to militia service. In Houston v. Moore, 5 Wheat. 1, 24 (1820), this Court held that States have concurrent power over the militia, at least where not pre-empted by Congress. Agreeing in dissent that States could "organize, discipline, and arm" the militia in the absence of conflicting federal regulation, Justice Story said that the Second Amendment "may not, perhaps, be thought to have any important bearing on this point. If it have, it confirms and illustrates, rather than impugns the reasoning already suggested." Id., at 51-53. Of course, if the Amendment simply "protect[ed] the right of the people of each of the several States to maintain a well-regulated militia," post, at 1 (STEVENS, J., dissenting), it would have enormous and obvious bearing on the point. But the Court and Story derived the States' power over the militia from the nonexclusive nature of federal power, not from the Second Amendment, whose preamble merely "confirms and illustrates" the importance of the militia. Even clearer was Justice Baldwin. In the famous fugitive-slave case of Johnson v. Tompkins, 13 F. Cas. 840, 850, 852 (CC Pa. 1833),

Baldwin, sitting as a circuit judge, cited both the Second Amendment and the Pennsylvania analogue for his conclusion that a citizen has "a right to carry arms in defence of his property or person, and to use them, if either were assailed with such force, numbers or violence as made it necessary for the protection or safety of either."

Many early 19th-century state cases indicated that the Second Amendment right to bear arms was an individual right unconnected to militia service, though subject to certain restrictions. A Virginia case in 1824 holding that the Constitution did not extend to free blacks explained that "numerous restrictions imposed on [blacks] in our Statute Book, many of which are inconsistent with the letter and spirit of the Constitution, both of this State and of the United States as respects the free whites, demonstrate, that, here, those instruments have not been considered to extend equally to both classes of our population. We will only instance the restriction upon the migration of free blacks into this State, and upon their right to bear arms." Aldridge v. Commonwealth, 2 Va. Cas. 447, 449 (Gen. Ct.). The claim was obviously not that blacks were prevented from carrying guns in the militia.21 See also Waters v. State, 1 Gill 302, 309 (Md. 1843) (because free blacks were treated as a "dangerous population," "laws have been passed to prevent their migration into this State; to make it unlawful for them to bear arms; to guard even their religious assemblages with peculiar watchfulness"). An 1829 decision by the Supreme Court of Michigan said: "The constitution of the United States also grants to the citizen the right to keep and bear arms. But the grant of this privilege cannot be construed into the right in him who keeps a gun to destroy his neighbor. No rights are intended to be granted by the constitution for an unlawful or unjustifiable purpose." United States v. Sheldon, in 5 Transactions of the Supreme Court of the Territory of Michigan 337, 346 (W. Blume ed. 1940) (hereinafter Blume). It is not possible to read this as discussing anything other than an individual right unconnected to militia service. If it did have to do with militia service, the limitation upon it would not be any "unlawful or unjustifiable purpose," but any nonmilitary purpose whatsoever.

In Nunn v. State, 1 Ga. 243, 251 (1846), the Georgia Supreme Court construed the Second Amendment as protecting the "natural right of self-defence" and therefore struck down a ban on carrying pistols openly. Its opinion perfectly captured the way in which the operative clause of the Second Amendment furthers the purpose announced in the prefatory clause, in continuity with the English right:

"The right of the whole people, old and young, men, women and boys, and not militia only, to keep and bear arms of every description, and not such merely as are used by the militia, shall not be infringed, curtailed, or broken in upon, in the smallest degree; and all this for the important end to be attained: the rearing up and qualifying a well-regulated militia, so vitally necessary to the security of a free State. Our opinion is, that any law, State or Federal, is repugnant to the Constitution, and void, which contravenes this right, originally belonging to our forefathers, trampled under foot by Charles I. and his two wicked sons and successors, re-established by the revolution of 1688, conveyed to this land of liberty by the colonists, and finally incorporated conspicuously in our own Magna Charta!"

Likewise, in State v. Chandler, 5 La. Ann. 489, 490 (1850), the Louisiana Supreme Court held that citizens had a right to carry arms openly: "This is the right guaranteed by the Constitution of the United States, and which is calculated to incite men to a manly and noble defence of themselves, if necessary, and of their country, without any tendency to secret advantages and unmanly assassinations."

Those who believe that the Second Amendment preserves only a militia-centered right place great reliance on the Tennessee Supreme Court's 1840 decision in Aymette v. State, 21 Tenn. 154. The case does not stand for that broad proposition; in fact, the case does not mention the word "militia" at all, except in its quoting of the Second Amendment. Aymette held that the state constitutional guarantee of the right to "bear" arms did not prohibit the banning of concealed weapons. The opinion first recognized that both the state right and the federal right were descendents of the 1689 English right, but (erroneously, and contrary to virtually all other authorities) read that right to refer only to "protect[ion of] the public liberty" and "keep[ing] in awe those in power," id., at 158. The court then adopted a sort of middle position, whereby citizens were permitted to carry arms openly, unconnected with any service in a formal militia, but were given the right to use them only for the military purpose of banding together to oppose tyranny. This odd reading of the right is, to be sure, not the one we adopt--but it is not petitioners' reading either. More importantly, seven years earlier the Tennessee Supreme Court had treated the state constitutional provision as conferring a right "of all the free citizens of the State to keep and bear arms for their defence," Simpson, 5 Yer., at 360; and 21 years later the court held that the "keep" portion of the state constitutional right included the right to personal self-defense: "[T]he right to keep arms involves, necessarily, the right to use such arms for all the ordinary purposes, and in all the ordinary modes usual in the country, and to which arms are adapted, limited by the duties of a good citizen in times of peace." Andrews, 50 Tenn., at 178; see also ibid. (equating state provision with Second Amendment).

3. Post-Civil War Legislation.

In the aftermath of the Civil War, there was an outpouring of discussion of the Second Amendment in Congress and in public discourse, as people debated whether and how to secure constitutional rights for newly free slaves. See generally S. Halbrook, Freedmen, the Fourteenth Amendment, and the Right to Bear Arms, 1866-1876 (1998) (hereinafter Halbrook); Brief for Institute for Justice as Amicus Curiae. Since those discussions took place 75 years after the ratification of the Second Amendment, they do not provide as much insight into its original meaning as earlier sources. Yet those born and educated in the early 19th century faced a widespread effort to limit arms ownership by a large number of citizens; their understanding of the origins and continuing significance of the Amendment is instructive.

Blacks were routinely disarmed by Southern States after the Civil War. Those who opposed these injustices frequently stated that they infringed blacks' constitutional right to keep and bear arms. Needless to say, the claim was not that blacks were being prohibited from carrying arms in an organized state militia. A Report of the Commission of the Freedmen's Bureau in 1866 stated plainly: "[T]he civil law [of Kentucky] prohibits the colored man from bearing arms. . . . Their arms are taken from them by the civil authorities... . Thus, the right of the people to keep and bear arms as provided in the Constitution is infringed." H. R. Exec. Doc. No. 70, 39th Cong., 1st Sess., 233, 236. A joint congressional Report decried:

"in some parts of [South Carolina], armed parties are, without proper authority, engaged in seizing all fire-arms found in the hands of the freemen. Such conduct is in clear and direct violation of their personal rights as guaranteed by the Constitution of the United States, which declares that 'the right of the people to keep and bear arms shall not be infringed.' The freedmen of South Carolina have shown by their peaceful and orderly conduct that they can safely be trusted with fire-arms, and they need them to kill game for subsistence, and to protect their crops from destruction by birds and animals." Joint Comm. on Reconstruction, H. R. Rep. No. 30, 39th Cong., 1st Sess., pt. 2, p. 229 (1866) (Proposed Circular of Brigadier General R. Saxton).

The view expressed in these statements was widely reported and was apparently widely held. For example, an editorial in The Loyal Georgian (Augusta) on February 3, 1866, assured blacks that "[a]ll men, without distinction of color, have the right to keep and bear arms to defend their homes, families or themselves." Halbrook 19.

Congress enacted the Freedmen's Bureau Act on July 16, 1866. Section 14 stated:

"[T]he right ... to have full and equal benefit of all laws and proceedings concerning personal liberty, personal security, and the acquisition, enjoyment, and disposition of estate, real and personal, including the constitutional right to bear arms, shall be secured to and enjoyed by all the citizens ... without respect to race or color, or previous condition of slavery.... " 14 Stat. 176-177.

The understanding that the Second Amendment gave freed blacks the right to keep and bear arms was reflected in congressional discussion of the bill, with even an opponent of it saying that the founding generation "were for every man bearing his arms about him and keeping them in his house, his castle, for his own defense." Cong. Globe, 39th Cong., 1st Sess., 362, 371 (1866) (Sen. Davis).

Similar discussion attended the passage of the Civil Rights Act of 1871 and the Fourteenth Amendment. For example, Representative Butler said of the Act: "Section eight is intended to enforce the well-known constitutional provision guaranteeing the right of the citizen to 'keep and bear arms,' and provides that whoever shall take away, by force or violence, or by threats and intimidation, the arms and weapons which any person may have for his defense, shall be deemed guilty of larceny of the same." H. R. Rep. No. 37, 41st Cong., 3d Sess., pp. 7-8 (1871). With respect to the proposed Amendment, Senator Pomeroy described as one of the three "indispensable" "safeguards of liberty ... under the Constitution" a man's "right to bear arms for the defense of himself and family and his homestead." Cong. Globe, 39th Cong., 1st Sess., 1182 (1866). Representative Nye thought the Fourteenth Amendment unnecessary because "[a]s citizens of the United States [blacks] have equal right to protection, and to keep and bear arms for self-defense." Id., at 1073 (1866).

It was plainly the understanding in the post-Civil War Congress that the Second Amendment protected an individual right to use arms for self-defense.

4. Post-Civil War Commentators.

Every late-19th-century legal scholar that we have read interpreted the Second Amendment to secure an individual right unconnected with militia service. The most famous was the judge and professor Thomas Cooley, who wrote a massively popular 1868 Treatise on Constitutional Limitations. Concerning the Second Amendment it said:

"Among the other defences to personal liberty should be mentioned the right of the people to keep and bear arms... . The alternative to a standing army is 'a well-regulated militia,' but this cannot exist unless the people are trained to bearing arms. How far it is in the power of the legislature to regulate this right, we shall not undertake to say, as happily there has been very little occasion to discuss that subject by the courts." Id., at 350.

That Cooley understood the right not as connected to militia service, but as securing the militia by ensuring a populace familiar with arms, is made even clearer in his 1880 work, General Principles of Constitutional Law. The Second Amendment, he said, "was adopted with some modification and enlargement from the English Bill of Rights of 1688, where it stood as a protest against arbitrary action of the overturned dynasty in disarming the people." Id., at 270. In a section entitled "The Right in General," he continued:

"It might be supposed from the phraseology of this provision that the right to keep and bear arms was only guaranteed to the militia; but this would be an interpretation not warranted by the intent. The militia, as has been elsewhere explained, consists of those persons who, under the law, are liable to the performance of military duty, and are officered and enrolled for service when called upon. But the law may make provision for the enrolment of all who are fit to perform military duty, or of a small number only, or it may wholly omit to make any provision at all; and if the right were limited to those enrolled, the purpose of this guaranty might be defeated altogether by the action or neglect to act of the government it was meant to hold in check. The meaning of the provision undoubtedly is, that the people, from whom the militia must be taken, shall have the right to keep and bear arms; and they need no permission or regulation of law for the purpose. But this enables government to have a well-regulated militia; for to bear arms implies something more than the mere keeping; it implies the learning to handle and use them in a way that makes those who keep them ready for their efficient use; in other words, it implies the right to meet for voluntary discipline in arms, observing in doing so the laws of public order." Id., at 271.

All other post-Civil War 19th-century sources we have found concurred with Cooley. One example from each decade will convey the general flavor:

"[The purpose of the Second Amendment is] to secure a well-armed militia... . But a militia would be useless unless the citizens were enabled to exercise themselves in the use of warlike weapons. To preserve this privilege, and to secure to the people the ability to oppose themselves in military force against the usurpations of government, as well as against enemies from without, that government is forbidden by any law or proceeding to invade or destroy the right to keep and bear arms... . The clause is analogous to the one securing the freedom of speech and of the press. Freedom, not license, is secured; the fair use, not the libellous abuse, is protected." J. Pomeroy, An Introduction to the Constitutional Law of the United States 152-153 (1868) (hereinafter Pomeroy).

"As the Constitution of the United States, and the constitutions of several of the states, in terms more or less comprehensive, declare the right of the people to keep and bear arms, it has been a subject of grave discussion, in some of the state courts, whether a statute prohibiting persons, when not on a journey, or as travellers, from wearing or carrying concealed weapons, be constitutional. There has been a great difference of opinion on the question." 2 J. Kent, Commentaries on American Law *340, n. 2 (O. Holmes ed., 12th ed. 1873) (hereinafter Kent).

"Some general knowledge of firearms is important to the public welfare; because it would be impossible, in case of war, to organize promptly an efficient force of volunteers unless the people had some familiarity with weapons of war. The Constitution secures the right of the people to keep and bear arms. No doubt, a citizen who keeps a gun or pistol under judicious precautions, practices in safe places the use of it, and in due time teaches his sons to do the same, exercises his individual right. No doubt, a person whose residence or duties involve peculiar peril may keep a pistol for prudent self-defence." B. Abbott, Judge and Jury: A Popular Explanation of the Leading Topics in the Law of the Land 333 (1880) (hereinafter Abbott).

"The right to bear arms has always been the distinctive privilege of freemen. Aside from any necessity of self-protection to the person, it represents among all nations power coupled with the exercise of a certain jurisdiction. ... [I]t was not necessary that the right to bear arms should be granted in the Constitution, for it had always existed." J. Ordronaux, Constitutional Legislation in the United States 241-242 (1891).

E

We now ask whether any of our precedents forecloses the conclusions we have reached about the meaning of the Second Amendment.

United States v. Cruikshank, 92 U. S. 542, in the course of vacating the convictions of members of a white mob for depriving blacks of their right to keep and bear arms, held that the Second Amendment does not by its own force apply to anyone other than the Federal Government. The opinion explained that the right "is not a right granted by the Constitution [or] in any manner dependent upon that instrument for its existence. The second amendment ... means no more than that it shall not be infringed by Congress." 92 U. S., at 553. States, we said, were free to restrict or protect the right under their police powers. The limited discussion of the Second Amendment in Cruikshank supports, if anything, the individual-rights interpretation. There was no claim in Cruikshank that the victims had been deprived of their right to carry arms in a militia; indeed, the Governor had disbanded the local militia unit the year before the mob's attack, see C. Lane, The Day Freedom Died 62 (2008). We described the right protected by the Second Amendment as " 'bearing arms for a lawful purpose' "22 and said that "the people [must] look for their protection against any violation by their fellow-citizens of the rights it recognizes" to the States' police power. 92 U.

S., at 553. That discussion makes little sense if it is only a right to bear arms in a state militia.23

Presser v. Illinois, 116 U. S. 252 (1886), held that the right to keep and bear arms was not violated by a law that forbade "bodies of men to associate together as military organizations, or to drill or parade with arms in cities and towns unless authorized by law." Id., at 264-265. This does not refute the individual-rights interpretation of the Amendment; no one supporting that interpretation has contended that States may not ban such groups. JUSTICE STEVENS presses Presser into service to support his view that the right to bear arms is limited to service in the militia by joining Presser's brief discussion of the Second Amendment with a later portion of the opinion making the seemingly relevant (to the Second Amendment) point that the plaintiff was not a member of the state militia. Unfortunately for JUSTICE STEVENS' argument, that later portion deals with the Fourteenth Amendment; it was the Fourteenth Amendment to which the plaintiff's nonmembership in the militia was relevant. Thus, JUSTICE STEVENS' statement that Presser "suggested that... nothing in the Constitution protected the use of arms outside the context of a militia," post, at 40, is simply wrong. Presser said nothing about the Second Amendment's meaning or scope, beyond the fact that it does not prevent the prohibition of private paramilitary organizations.

JUSTICE STEVENS places overwhelming reliance upon this Court's decision in United States v. Miller, 307 U. S. 174 (1939). "[H]undreds of judges," we are told, "have relied on the view of the amendment we endorsed there," post, at 2, and "[e]ven if the textual and historical arguments on both side of the issue were evenly balanced, respect for the well-settled views of all of our predecessors on this Court, and for the rule of law itself ... would prevent most jurists from endorsing such a dramatic upheaval in the law," post, at 4. And what is, according to JUSTICE STEVENS, the holding of Miller that demands such obeisance? That the Second Amendment "protects the right to keep and bear arms for certain military purposes, but that it does not curtail the legislature's power to regulate the nonmilitary use and ownership of weapons." Post, at 2.

Nothing so clearly demonstrates the weakness of JUSTICE STEVENS' case. Miller did not hold that and cannot possibly be read to have held that. The judgment in the case upheld against a Second Amendment challenge two men's federal convictions for transporting an unregistered short-barreled shotgun in interstate commerce, in violation of the National Firearms Act, 48 Stat. 1236. It is entirely clear that the Court's basis for saying that the Second Amendment did not apply was not that the defendants were "bear[ing] arms" not "for ... military purposes" but for "nonmilitary use," post, at 2. Rather, it was that the type of weapon at issue was not eligible for Second Amendment protection: "In the absence of any evidence tending to show that the possession or use of a [short-barreled shotgun] at this time has some reasonable relationship to the preservation or efficiency of a well regulated militia, we cannot say that the Second Amendment guarantees the right to keep and bear such an instrument." 307 U. S., at

178 (emphasis added). "Certainly," the Court continued, "it is not within judicial notice that this weapon is any part of the ordinary military equipment or that its use could contribute to the common defense." Ibid. Beyond that, the opinion provided no explanation of the content of the right.

This holding is not only consistent with, but positively suggests, that the Second Amendment confers an individual right to keep and bear arms (though only arms that "have some reasonable relationship to the preservation or efficiency of a well regulated militia"). Had the Court believed that the Second Amendment protects only those serving in the militia, it would have been odd to examine the character of the weapon rather than simply note that the two crooks were not militiamen. JUSTICE STEVENS can say again and again that Miller did "not turn on the difference between muskets and sawed-off shotguns, it turned, rather, on the basic difference between the military and nonmilitary use and possession of guns," post, at 42-43, but the words of the opinion prove otherwise. The most JUSTICE STEVENS can plausibly claim for Miller is that it declined to decide the nature of the Second Amendment right, despite the Solicitor General's argument (made in the alternative) that the right was collective, see Brief for United States, O. T. 1938, No. 696, pp. 4-5. Miller stands only for the proposition that the Second Amendment right, whatever its nature, extends only to certain types of weapons.

It is particularly wrongheaded to read Miller for more than what it said, because the case did not even purport to be a thorough examination of the Second Amendment. JUSTICE STEVENS claims, post, at 42, that the opinion reached its conclusion "[a]fter reviewing many of the same sources that are discussed at greater length by the Court today." Not many, which was not entirely the Court's fault. The respondent made no appearance in the case, neither filing a brief nor appearing at oral argument; the Court heard from no one but the Government (reason enough, one would think, not to make that case the beginning and the end of this Court's consideration of the Second Amendment). See Frye, The Peculiar Story of United States v. Miller, 3 N. Y. U. J. L. & Liberty 48, 65-68 (2008). The Government's brief spent two pages discussing English legal sources, concluding "that at least the carrying of weapons without lawful occasion or excuse was always a crime" and that (because of the class-based restrictions and the prohibition on terrorizing people with dangerous or unusual weapons) "the early English law did not guarantee an unrestricted right to bear arms." Brief for United States, O. T. 1938, No. 696, at 9-11. It then went on to rely primarily on the discussion of the English right to bear arms in Aymette v. State, 21 Tenn. 154, for the proposition that the only uses of arms protected by the Second Amendment are those that relate to the militia, not self-defense. See Brief for United States, O. T. 1938, No. 696, at 12-18. The final section of the brief recognized that "some courts have said that the right to bear arms includes the right of the individual to have them for the protection of his person and property," and launched an alternative argument that "weapons which are commonly used by criminals," such as sawed-off shotguns, are not protected. See id., at 18-21.

The Government's Miller brief thus provided scant discussion of the history of the Second Amendment--and the Court was presented with no counterdiscussion. As for the text of the Court's opinion itself, that discusses none of the history of the Second Amendment. It assumes from the prologue that the Amendment was designed to preserve the militia, 307 U. S., at 178 (which we do not dispute), and then reviews some historical materials dealing with the nature of the militia, and in particular with the nature of the arms their members were expected to possess, id., at 178-182. Not a word (not a word) about the history of the Second Amendment. This is the mighty rock upon which the dissent rests its case.24

We may as well consider at this point (for we will have to consider eventually) what types of weapons Miller permits. Read in isolation, Miller's phrase "part of ordinary military equipment" could mean that only those weapons useful in warfare are protected. That would be a startling reading of the opinion, since it would mean that the National Firearms Act's restrictions on machineguns (not challenged in Miller) might be unconstitutional, machineguns being useful in warfare in 1939. We think that Miller's "ordinary military equipment" language must be read in tandem with what comes after: "[O]rdinarily when called for [militia] service [able-bodied] men were expected to appear bearing arms supplied by themselves and of the kind in common use at the time." 307 U. S., at 179. The traditional militia was formed from a pool of men bringing arms "in common use at the time" for lawful purposes like self-defense. "In the colonial and revolutionary war era, [small-arms] weapons used by militiamen and weapons used in defense of person and home were one and the same." State v. Kessler, 289 Ore. 359, 368, 614 P. 2d 94, 98 (1980) (citing G. Neumann, Swords and Blades of the American Revolution 6-15, 252-254 (1973)). Indeed, that is precisely the way in which the Second Amendment's operative clause furthers the purpose announced in its preface. We therefore read Miller to say only that the Second Amendment does not protect those weapons not typically possessed by law-abiding citizens for lawful purposes, such as short-barreled shotguns. That accords with the historical understanding of the scope of the right, see Part III, infra.25

We conclude that nothing in our precedents forecloses our adoption of the original understanding of the Second Amendment. It should be unsurprising that such a significant matter has been for so long judicially unresolved. For most of our history, the Bill of Rights was not thought applicable to the States, and the Federal Government did not significantly regulate the possession of firearms by law-abiding citizens. Other provisions of the Bill of Rights have similarly remained unilluminated for lengthy periods. This Court first held a law to violate the First Amendment's guarantee of freedom of speech in 1931, almost 150 years after the Amendment was ratified, see Near v. Minnesota ex rel. Olson, 283 U. S. 697 (1931), and it was not until after World War II that we held a law invalid under the Establishment Clause, see Illinois ex rel. McCollum v. Board of Ed. of School Dist. No. 71, Champaign Cty., 333 U. S. 203 (1948). Even a question as basic as the scope of proscribable libel was not addressed by this Court until 1964, nearly two centuries after the founding. See New York Times Co. v. Sullivan, 376 U. S. 254 (1964). It is demonstrably not true that, as JUSTICE STEVENS claims, post, at 41-42, "for most of our history, the invalidity of Second-Amendment-based objections to firearms regulations has been well settled and uncontroversial." For most of our history the question did not present itself.

III

Like most rights, the right secured by the Second Amendment is not unlimited. From Blackstone through the 19th-century cases, commentators and courts routinely explained that the right was not a right to keep and carry any weapon whatsoever in any manner whatsoever and for whatever purpose. See, e.g., Sheldon, in 5 Blume 346; Rawle 123; Pomeroy 152-153; Abbott 333. For example, the majority of the 19th-century courts to consider the question held that prohibitions on carrying concealed weapons were lawful under the Second Amendment or state analogues. See, e.g., State v. Chandler, 5 La. Ann., at 489-490; Nunn v. State, 1 Ga., at 251; see generally 2 Kent *340, n. 2; The American Students' Blackstone 84, n. 11 (G. Chase ed. 1884). Although we do not undertake an exhaustive historical analysis today of the full scope of the Second Amendment, nothing in our opinion should be taken to cast doubt on longstanding prohibitions on the possession of firearms by felons and the mentally ill, or laws forbidding the carrying of firearms in sensitive places such as schools and government buildings, or laws imposing conditions and qualifications on the commercial sale of arms.26

We also recognize another important limitation on the right to keep and carry arms. Miller said, as we have explained, that the sorts of weapons protected were those "in common use at the time." 307 U. S., at 179. We think that limitation is fairly supported by the historical tradition of prohibiting the carrying of "dangerous and unusual weapons." See 4 Blackstone 148-149 (1769); 3 B. Wilson, Works of the Honourable James Wilson 79 (1804); J. Dunlap, The New-York Justice 8 (1815); C. Humphreys, A Compendium of the Common Law in Force in Kentucky 482 (1822); 1 W. Russell, A Treatise on Crimes and Indictable Misdemeanors 271-272 (1831); H. Stephen, Summary of the Criminal Law 48 (1840); E. Lewis, An Abridgment of the Criminal Law of the United States 64 (1847); F. Wharton, A Treatise on the Criminal Law of the United States 726 (1852). See also State v. Langford, 10 N. C. 381, 383-384 (1824); O'Neill v. State, 16 Ala. 65, 67 (1849); English v. State, 35 Tex. 473, 476 (1871); State v. Lanier, 71 N. C. 288, 289 (1874).

It may be objected that if weapons that are most useful in military service--M-16 rifles and the like--may be banned, then the Second Amendment right is completely detached from the prefatory clause. But as we have said, the conception of the militia at the time of the Second Amendment's ratification was the body of all citizens capable of military service, who would bring the sorts of lawful weapons that they possessed at home to militia duty. It may well be true today that a militia, to be as effective as militias in the 18th century, would require sophisticated arms that are highly unusual in society at large. Indeed, it may be true that no amount of small arms could be useful against modern-day bombers and tanks. But the fact that modern developments have limited the degree of fit between the prefatory clause and the protected right cannot change our interpretation of the right.

IV

We turn finally to the law at issue here. As we have said, the law totally bans handgun possession in the home. It also requires that any lawful firearm in the home be disassembled or bound by a trigger lock at all times, rendering it inoperable.

As the quotations earlier in this opinion demonstrate, the inherent right of self-defense has been central to the Second Amendment right. The handgun ban amounts to a prohibition of an entire class of "arms" that is overwhelmingly chosen by American society for that lawful purpose. The prohibition extends, moreover, to the home, where the need for defense of self, family, and property is most acute. Under any of the standards of scrutiny that we have applied to enumerated constitutional rights,27 banning from the home "the most preferred firearm in the nation to 'keep' and use for protection of one's home and family," 478 F. 3d, at 400, would fail constitutional muster.

BAN ASSAULT BANANAS

Few laws in the history of our Nation have come close to the severe restriction of the District's handgun ban. And some of those few have been struck down. In Nunn v. State, the Georgia Supreme Court struck down a prohibition on carrying pistols openly (even though it upheld a prohibition on carrying concealed weapons). See 1 Ga., at 251. In Andrews v. State, the Tennessee Supreme Court likewise held that a statute that forbade openly carrying a pistol "publicly or privately, without regard to time or place, or circumstances," 50 Tenn., at 187, violated the state constitutional provision (which the court equated with the Second Amendment). That was so even though the statute did not restrict the carrying of long guns. Ibid. See also State v. Reid, 1 Ala. 612, 616-617 (1840) ("A statute which, under the pretence of regulating, amounts to a destruction of the right, or which requires arms to be so borne as to render them wholly useless for the purpose of defence, would be clearly unconstitutional").

It is no answer to say, as petitioners do, that it is permissible to ban the possession of handguns so long as the possession of other firearms (i.e., long guns) is allowed. It is enough to note, as we have observed, that the American people have considered the handgun to be the quintessential self-defense weapon. There are many reasons that a citizen may prefer a handgun for home defense: It is easier to store in a location that is readily accessible in an emergency; it cannot easily be redirected or wrestled away by an attacker; it is easier to use for those without the upper-body strength to lift and aim a long gun; it can be pointed at a burglar with one hand while the other hand dials the police. Whatever the reason, handguns are the most popular weapon chosen by Americans for self-defense in the home, and a complete prohibition of their use is invalid.

We must also address the District's requirement (as applied to respondent's handgun) that firearms in the home be rendered and kept inoperable at all times. This makes it impossible for citizens to use them for the core lawful purpose of self-defense and is hence unconstitutional. The District argues that we should interpret this element of the statute to contain an exception for self-defense. See Brief for Petitioners 56-57. But we think that is precluded by the unequivocal text, and by the presence of certain other enumerated exceptions: "Except for law enforcement personnel ... , each registrant shall keep any firearm in his possession unloaded and disassembled or bound by a trigger lock or similar device unless such firearm is kept at his place of business, or while being used for lawful recreational purposes within the District of Columbia." D. C. Code §7-2507.02. The nonexistence of a self-defense exception is also suggested by the D. C. Court of Appeals' statement that the statute forbids residents to use firearms to stop intruders, see McIntosh v. Washington, 395 A. 2d 744, 755-756 (1978).28

Apart from his challenge to the handgun ban and the trigger-lock requirement respondent asked the District Court to enjoin petitioners from enforcing the separate licensing requirement "in such a manner as to forbid the carrying of a firearm within one's home or possessed land without a license." App. 59a. The Court of Appeals did not invalidate the licensing requirement, but held only that the District "may not prevent [a handgun] from being moved throughout one's house." 478 F. 3d, at 400. It then ordered the District Court to enter summary judgment "consistent with [respondent's] prayer for relief." Id., at 401. Before this Court petitioners have stated that "if the handgun ban is struck down and respondent registers a handgun, he could obtain a license, assuming he is not otherwise disqualified," by which they apparently mean if he is not a felon and is not insane. Brief for Petitioners 58. Respondent conceded at oral argument that he does not "have a problem with ... licensing" and that the District's law is permissible so long as it is "not enforced in an arbitrary and capricious manner." Tr. of Oral Arg. 74-75. We therefore assume that petitioners' issuance of a license will satisfy respondent's prayer for relief and do not address the licensing requirement.

JUSTICE BREYER has devoted most of his separate dissent to the handgun ban. He says that, even assuming the Second Amendment is a personal guarantee of the right to bear arms, the District's prohibition is valid. He first tries to establish this by founding-era historical precedent, pointing to various restrictive laws in the colonial period. These demonstrate, in his view, that the District's law "imposes a burden upon gun owners that seems proportionately no greater than restrictions in existence at the time the Second Amendment was adopted." Post, at 2. Of the laws he cites, only one offers even marginal support for his assertion. A 1783 Massachusetts law forbade the residents of Boston to "take into" or "receive into" "any Dwelling House, Stable, Barn, Out-house, Ware-house, Store, Shop or other Building" loaded firearms, and permitted the seizure of any loaded firearms that "shall be found" there. Act of Mar. 1, 1783, ch. 13, 1783 Mass. Acts p. 218. That statute's text and its prologue, which makes clear that the purpose of the prohibition was to eliminate the danger to firefighters posed by the "depositing of loaded Arms" in buildings, give reason to doubt that colonial Boston authorities would have enforced that general prohibition against someone who temporarily loaded a firearm to confront an intruder (despite the law's application in that case). In any case, we would not stake our interpretation of the Second Amendment upon a single law, in effect in a single city, that contradicts the overwhelming weight of other evidence regarding the right to keep and bear arms for defense of the home. The other laws JUSTICE BREYER cites are gunpowder-storage laws that he concedes did not clearly prohibit loaded weapons, but required only that excess gunpowder be kept in a special container or on the top floor of the home. Post, at 6-7. Nothing about those fire-safety laws undermines our analysis; they do not remotely burden the right of self-defense as much as an absolute ban on handguns. Nor, correspondingly, does our analysis suggest the invalidity of laws regulating the storage of firearms to prevent accidents.

JUSTICE BREYER points to other founding-era laws that he says "restricted the firing of guns within the city limits to at least some degree" in Boston, Philadelphia and New

York. Post, at 4 (citing Churchill, Gun Regulation, the Police Power, and the Right to Keep Arms in Early America, 25 Law & Hist. Rev. 139, 162 (2007)). Those laws provide no support for the severe restriction in the present case. The New York law levied a fine of 20 shillings on anyone who fired a gun in certain places (including houses) on New Year's Eve and the first two days of January, and was aimed at preventing the "great Damages ... frequently done on [those days] by persons going House to House, with Guns and other Firearms and being often intoxicated with Liquor." 5 Colonial Laws of New York 244-246 (1894). It is inconceivable that this law would have been enforced against a person exercising his right to self-defense on New Year's Day against such drunken hooligans. The Pennsylvania law to which JUSTICE BREYER refers levied a fine of 5 shillings on one who fired a gun or set off fireworks in Philadelphia without first obtaining a license from the governor. See Act of Aug. 26, 1721, §4, in 3 Stat. at Large 253-254. Given Justice Wilson's explanation that the right to self-defense with arms was protected by the Pennsylvania Constitution, it is unlikely that this law (which in any event amounted to at most a licensing regime) would have been enforced against a person who used firearms for self-defense. JUSTICE BREYER cites a Rhode Island law that simply levied a 5-shilling fine on those who fired guns in streets and taverns, a law obviously inapplicable to this case. See An Act for preventing Mischief being done in the town of Newport, or in any other town in this Government, 1731, Rhode Island Session Laws. Finally, JUSTICE BREYER points to a Massachusetts law similar to the Pennsylvania law, prohibiting "discharg[ing] any Gun or Pistol charged with Shot or Ball in the Town of Boston." Act of May 28, 1746, ch. X, Acts and Laws of Mass. Bay 208. It is again implausible that this would have been enforced against a citizen acting in self-defense, particularly given its preambulatory reference to "the indiscreet firing of Guns." Ibid. (preamble) (emphasis added).

A broader point about the laws that JUSTICE BREYER cites: All of them punished the discharge (or loading) of guns with a small fine and forfeiture of the weapon (or in a few cases a very brief stay in the local jail), not with significant criminal penalties.29 They are akin to modern penalties for minor public-safety infractions like speeding or jaywalking. And although such public-safety laws may not contain exceptions for self-defense, it is inconceivable that the threat of a jaywalking ticket would deter someone from disregarding a "Do Not Walk" sign in order to flee an attacker, or that the Government would enforce those laws under such circumstances. Likewise, we do not think that a law imposing a 5-shilling fine and forfeiture of the gun would have prevented a person in the founding era from using a gun to protect himself or his family from violence, or that if he did so the law would be enforced against him. The District law, by contrast, far from imposing a minor fine, threatens citizens with a year in prison (five years for a second violation) for even obtaining a gun in the first place. See D. C. Code §7-2507.06.

JUSTICE BREYER moves on to make a broad jurisprudential point: He criticizes us for declining to establish a level of scrutiny for evaluating Second

Amendment restrictions. He proposes, explicitly at least, none of the traditionally expressed levels (strict scrutiny, intermediate scrutiny, rational basis), but rather a judge-empowering "interest-balancing inquiry" that "asks whether the statute burdens a protected interest in a way or to an extent that is out of proportion to the statute's salutary effects upon other important governmental interests." Post, at 10. After an exhaustive discussion of the arguments for and against gun control, JUSTICE BREYER arrives at his interest-balanced answer: because handgun violence is a problem, because the law is limited to an urban area, and because there were somewhat similar restrictions in the founding period (a false proposition that we have already discussed), the interest-balancing inquiry results in the constitutionality of the handgun ban. QED.

We know of no other enumerated constitutional right whose core protection has been subjected to a freestanding "interest-balancing" approach. The very enumeration of the right takes out of the hands of government--even the Third Branch of Government--the power to decide on a case-by-case basis whether the right is really worth insisting upon. A constitutional guarantee subject to future judges' assessments of its usefulness is no constitutional guarantee at all. Constitutional rights are enshrined with the scope they were understood to have when the people adopted them, whether or not future legislatures or (yes) even future judges think that scope too broad. We would not apply an "interest-balancing" approach to the prohibition of a peaceful neo-Nazi march through Skokie. See National Socialist Party of America v. Skokie, 432 U. S. 43 (1977) (per curiam). The First Amendment contains the freedom-of-speech guarantee that the people ratified, which included exceptions for obscenity, libel, and disclosure of state secrets, but not for the expression of extremely unpopular and wrong-headed views. The Second Amendment is no different. Like the First, it is the very product of an interest-balancing by the people--which JUSTICE BREYER would now conduct for them anew. And whatever else it leaves to future evaluation, it surely elevates above all other interests the right of law-abiding, responsible citizens to use arms in defense of hearth and home.

JUSTICE BREYER chides us for leaving so many applications of the right to keep and bear arms in doubt, and for not providing extensive historical justification for those regulations of the right that we describe as permissible. See post, at 42-43. But since this case represents this Court's first in-depth examination of the Second Amendment, one should not expect it to clarify the entire field, any more than Reynolds v. United States, 98 U. S. 145 (1879), our first in-depth Free Exercise Clause case, left that area in a state of utter certainty. And there will be time enough to expound upon the historical justifications for the exceptions we have mentioned if and when those exceptions come before us.

In sum, we hold that the District's ban on handgun possession in the home violates the Second Amendment, as does its prohibition against rendering any lawful firearm in the home operable for the purpose of immediate self-defense. **Assuming that Heller is not disqualified from the exercise of Second Amendment rights,** the District must permit him to register his handgun and must issue him a license to carry it in the home.

* * *

We are aware of the problem of handgun violence in this country, and we take seriously the concerns raised by the many amici who believe that prohibition of handgun ownership is a solution. The Constitution leaves the District of Columbia a variety of tools for combating that problem, including some measures regulating handguns, see supra, at 54-55, and n. 26. But the enshrinement of constitutional rights necessarily takes certain policy choices off the table. These include the absolute prohibition of handguns held and used for self-defense in the home. Undoubtedly some think that the Second Amendment is outmoded in a society where our standing army is the pride of our Nation, where well-trained police forces provide personal security, and where gun violence is a serious problem. That is perhaps debatable, but what is not debatable is that it is not the role of this Court to pronounce the Second Amendment extinct.

We affirm the judgment of the Court of Appeals.

It is so ordered.

UNITED STATES
v.
Alfonso LOPEZ, Jr.

**No. 93-1260.
514 U.S. 549, 115 S.Ct. 1624
131 L.Ed.2d 626
Supreme Court of the United States
Argued Nov. 8, 1994.
Decided April 26, 1995.**

REHNQUIST, C.J., delivered the opinion of the Court, in which O'CONNOR, SCALIA, KENNEDY, and THOMAS, JJ., joined. KENNEDY, J., filed a concurring opinion, in which O'CONNOR, J., joined. THOMAS, J., filed a concurring opinion. STEVENS, J., and SOUTER, J., filed dissenting opinions. BREYER, J., filed a dissenting opinion, in which STEVENS, SOUTER, and GINSBURG, JJ., joined.

Drew S. Days, III, New Haven, CT, for petitioner.

John R. Carter, Georgetown, TX, for respondent.

Chief Justice REHNQUIST delivered the opinion of the Court.

In the Gun-Free School Zones Act of 1990, Congress made it a federal offense "for any individual knowingly to possess a firearm at a place that the individual knows, or has reasonable cause to believe, is a school zone." 18 U.S.C. § 922(q)(1)(A) (1988 ed., Supp. V). The Act neither regulates a commercial activity nor contains a requirement that the possession be connected in any way to interstate commerce. We hold that the Act exceeds the authority of Congress "[t]o regulate Commerce . . . among the several States. . . ." U.S. Const., Art. I, § 8, cl. 3.

On March 10, 1992, respondent, who was then a 12th-grade student, arrived at Edison High School in San Antonio, Texas, carrying a concealed .38 caliber handgun and five bullets. Acting upon an anonymous tip, school authorities confronted respondent, who admitted that he was carrying the weapon. He was arrested and charged under Texas law with firearm possession on school premises. See Tex.Penal Code Ann. § 46.03(a)(1) (Supp.1994). The next day, the state charges were dismissed after federal agents charged respondent by complaint with violating the Gun-Free School Zones Act of 1990. 18 U.S.C. § 922(q)(1)(A) (1988 ed., Supp. V).1

A federal grand jury indicted respondent on one count of knowing possession of a firearm at a school zone, in violation of § 922(q). Respondent moved to dismiss his federal indictment on the ground that § 922(q) "is unconstitutional as it is beyond the power of Congress to legislate control over our public schools." The District Court denied the motion, concluding that § 922(q) "is a constitutional exercise of Congress' well-defined power to regulate activities in and affecting commerce, and the 'business' of elementary, middle and high schools . . . affects interstate commerce." App. to Pet. for Cert. 55a. Respondent waived his right to a jury trial. The District Court conducted a bench trial, found him guilty of violating

§ 922(q), and sentenced him to six months' imprisonment and two years' supervised release.

On appeal, respondent challenged his conviction based on his claim that § 922(q) exceeded Congress' power to legislate under the Commerce Clause. The Court of Appeals for the Fifth Circuit agreed and reversed respondent's conviction. It held that, in light of what it characterized as insufficient congressional findings and legislative history, "section 922(q), in the full reach of its terms, is invalid as beyond the power of Congress under the Commerce Clause." 2 F.3d 1342, 1367-1368 (1993). Because of the importance of the issue, we granted certiorari, 511 U.S. ----, 114 S.Ct. 1536, 128 L.Ed.2d 189 (1994), and we now affirm.

We start with first principles. The Constitution creates a Federal Government of enumerated powers. See U.S. Const., Art. I, § 8. As James Madison wrote, "[t]he powers delegated by the proposed Constitution to the federal government are few and defined. Those which are to remain in the State governments are numerous and indefinite." The Federalist No. 45, pp. 292-293 (C. Rossiter ed. 1961). This constitutionally mandated division of authority "was adopted by the Framers to ensure protection of our fundamental liberties." Gregory v. Ashcroft, 501 U.S. 452, 458, 111 S.Ct. 2395, 2400, 115 L.Ed.2d 410 (1991) (internal quotation marks omitted). "Just as the separation and independence of the coordinate branches of the Federal Government serves to prevent the accumulation of excessive power in any one branch, a healthy balance of power between the States and the Federal Government will reduce the risk of tyranny and abuse from either front." Ibid.

BAN ASSAULT BANANAS

The Constitution delegates to Congress the power "[t]o regulate Commerce with foreign Nations, and among the several States, and with the Indian Tribes." U.S. Const., Art. I, § 8, cl. 3. The Court, through Chief Justice Marshall, first defined the nature of Congress' commerce power in Gibbons v. Ogden, 9 Wheat. 1, 189-190, 6 L.Ed. 23 (1824)

"Commerce, undoubtedly, is traffic, but it is something more: it is intercourse. It describes the commercial intercourse between nations, and parts of nations, in all its branches, and is regulated by prescribing rules for carrying on that intercourse."

The commerce power "is the power to regulate; that is, to prescribe the rule by which commerce is to be governed. This power, like all others vested in Congress, is complete in itself, may be exercised to its utmost extent, and acknowledges no limitations, other than are prescribed in the constitution." Id., at 196. The Gibbons Court, however, acknowledged that limitations on the commerce power are inherent in the very language of the Commerce Clause.
"It is not intended to say that these words comprehend that commerce, which is completely internal, which is carried on between man and man in a State, or between different parts of the same State, and which does not extend to or affect other States. Such a power would be inconvenient, and is certainly unnecessary.
"Comprehensive as the word 'among' is, it may very properly be restricted to that commerce which concerns more States than one. . . . The enumeration presupposes something not enumerated; and that something, if we

regard the language or the subject of the sentence, must be the exclusively internal commerce of a State." Id., at 194-195.

For nearly a century thereafter, the Court's Commerce Clause decisions dealt but rarely with the extent of Congress' power, and almost entirely with the Commerce Clause as a limit on state legislation that discriminated against interstate commerce. See, e.g., Veazie v. Moor, 14 How. 568, 573-575, 14 L.Ed. 545 (1853) (upholding a state-created steamboat monopoly because it involved regulation of wholly internal commerce); Kidd v. Pearson, 128 U.S. 1, 17, 20-22, 9 S.Ct. 6, 9-10, 32 L.Ed. 346 (1888) (upholding a state prohibition on the manufacture of intoxicating liquor because the commerce power "does not comprehend the purely domestic commerce of a State which is carried on between man and man within a State or between different parts of the same State"); see also L. Tribe, American Constitutional Law 306 (2d ed. 1988). Under this line of precedent, the Court held that certain categories of activity such as "production," "manufacturing," and "mining" were within the province of state governments, and thus were beyond the power of Congress under the Commerce Clause. See Wickard v. Filburn, 317 U.S. 111, 121, 63 S.Ct. 82, 87, 87 L.Ed. 122 (1942) (describing development of Commerce Clause jurisprudence).

In 1887, Congress enacted the Interstate Commerce Act, 24 Stat. 379, and in 1890, Congress enacted the Sherman Antitrust Act, 26 Stat. 209, as amended, 15 U.S.C. § 1 et seq. These laws ushered in a new era of federal regulation under the commerce power. When cases involving these laws first reached this Court, we imported from our negative Commerce Clause cases the approach that Congress could not regulate activities such as "production," "manufacturing," and "mining." See, e.g., United States v. E.C. Knight Co., 156 U.S. 1, 12, 15 S.Ct. 249, 253-254, 39 L.Ed. 325 (1895) ("Commerce succeeds to manufacture, and is not part of it"); Carter v. Carter Coal Co., 298 U.S. 238, 304, 56 S.Ct. 855, 869, 80 L.Ed. 1160 (1936) ("Mining brings the subject matter of commerce into existence. Commerce disposes of it"). Simultaneously, however, the Court held that, where the interstate and intrastate aspects of commerce were so mingled together that full regulation of interstate commerce required incidental regulation of intrastate commerce, the Commerce Clause authorized such regulation. See, e.g., Houston, E. & W.T.R. Co. v. United States, 234 U.S. 342, 34 S.Ct. 833, 58 L.Ed. 1341 (1914) (Shreveport Rate Cases).

In A.L.A. Schecter Poultry Corp. v. United States, 295 U.S. 495, 550, 55 S.Ct. 837, 851-52, 79 L.Ed. 1570 (1935), the Court struck down regulations that fixed the hours and wages of individuals employed by an intrastate business because the activity being regulated related to interstate commerce only indirectly. In doing so, the Court characterized the distinction between direct and indirect effects of intrastate transactions upon interstate commerce as "a fundamental one, essential to the maintenance of our constitutional system." Id., at 548, 55 S.Ct., at 851. Activities that affected interstate commerce directly were within Congress' power; activities that affected interstate commerce indirectly were beyond Congress' reach. Id., at 546, 55 S.Ct., at 850. The justification for this formal distinction was rooted in the fear that otherwise "there would be virtually no limit to the federal power and for all practical purposes we should have a completely centralized government." Id., at 548, 55 S.Ct., at 851.

Two years later, in the watershed case of NLRB v. Jones & Laughlin Steel Corp., 301 U.S. 1, 57 S.Ct. 615, 81 L.Ed. 893 (1937), the Court upheld the National Labor Relations Act against a Commerce Clause challenge, and in the process, departed from the distinction between "direct" and "indirect" effects on interstate commerce. Id., at 36-38, 57 S.Ct., at 623-624 ("The question [of the scope of Congress' power] is necessarily one of degree"). The Court held that intrastate activities that "have such a close and substantial relation to interstate commerce that their control is essential or appropriate to protect that commerce from burdens and obstructions" are within Congress' power to regulate. Id., at 37, 57 S.Ct., at 624.

In United States v. Darby, 312 U.S. 100, 61 S.Ct. 451, 85 L.Ed. 609 (1941), the Court upheld the Fair Labor Standards Act, stating:

"The power of Congress over interstate commerce is not confined to the regulation of commerce among the states. It extends to those activities intrastate which so affect interstate commerce or the exercise of the power of Congress over it as to make regulation of them appropriate means to the attainment of a legitimate end, the exercise of the granted power of Congress to regulate interstate commerce." Id., at 118, 61 S.Ct., at 459.

See also United States v. Wrightwood Dairy Co., 315 U.S. 110, 119, 62 S.Ct. 523, 526, 86 L.Ed. 726 (1942) (the commerce power "extends to those intrastate activities which in a substantial way interfere with or obstruct the exercise of the granted power").

In Wickard v. Filburn, the Court upheld the application of amendments to the Agricultural Adjustment Act of 1938 to the production and consumption of homegrown wheat. 317 U.S., at 128-129, 63 S.Ct., at 90-91. The Wickard Court explicitly rejected earlier distinctions between direct and indirect effects on interstate commerce, stating:

"[E]ven if appellee's activity be local and though it may not be regarded as commerce, it may still, whatever its nature, be reached by Congress if it exerts a substantial economic effect on interstate commerce, and this irrespective of whether such effect is what might at some earlier time have been defined as 'direct' or 'indirect.' " Id., at 125, 63 S.Ct., at 89.

The Wickard Court emphasized that although Filburn's own contribution to the demand for wheat may have been trivial by itself, that was not "enough to remove him from the scope of federal regulation where, as here, his contribution, taken together with that of many others similarly situated, is far from trivial." Id., at 127-128, 63 S.Ct., at 90-91.

Jones & Laughlin Steel, Darby, and Wickard ushered in an era of Commerce Clause jurisprudence that greatly expanded the previously defined authority of Congress under that Clause. In part, this was a recognition of the great changes that had occurred in the way business was carried on in this country. Enterprises that had once been local or at most regional in nature had become national in scope. But the doctrinal change also reflected a view that earlier Commerce Clause cases artificially had constrained the authority of Congress to regulate interstate commerce.

But even these modern-era precedents which have expanded congressional power under the Commerce Clause confirm that this power is subject to outer limits. In Jones & Laughlin Steel, the Court warned that the scope of the interstate commerce power "must be considered in the light of our dual system of government and may not be extended so as to embrace effects upon interstate commerce so indirect and remote that to embrace them, in view of our complex society, would effectually obliterate the distinction between what is national and what is local and create a completely centralized government." 301 U.S., at 37, 57 S.Ct., at 624; see also Darby, supra, 312 U.S., at 119-120, 61 S.Ct., at 459-460 (Congress may regulate intrastate activity that has a "substantial effect" on interstate commerce); Wickard, supra, at 125, 63 S.Ct., at 89 (Congress may regulate activity that "exerts a substantial economic effect on interstate commerce"). Since that time, the Court has heeded that warning and undertaken to decide whether a rational basis existed for concluding that a regulated activity sufficiently affected interstate commerce. See, e.g., Hodel v. Virginia Surface Mining & Reclamation Assn., Inc., 452 U.S. 264, 276-280, 101 S.Ct. 2352, 2360-2361, 69 L.Ed.2d 1 (1981); Perez v. United States, 402 U.S. 146, 155-156, 91 S.Ct. 1357, 1362, 28 L.Ed.2d 686 (1971); Katzenbach v. McClung, 379 U.S. 294, 299-301, 85 S.Ct. 377, 381-382, 13 L.Ed.2d 290 (1964); Heart of Atlanta Motel, Inc. v. United States, 379 U.S. 241, 252-253, 85 S.Ct. 348, 354-355, 13 L.Ed.2d 258 (1964).2

Similarly, in Maryland v. Wirtz, 392 U.S. 183, 88 S.Ct. 2017, 20 L.Ed.2d 1020 (1968), the Court reaffirmed that "the power to regulate commerce, though broad indeed, has limits" that "[t]he Court has ample power" to enforce. Id., at 196, 88 S.Ct., at 2023-2024, overruled on other grounds, National League of Cities v. Usery, 426 U.S. 833, 96 S.Ct. 2465, 49 L.Ed.2d 245 (1976), overruled by Garcia v. San Antonio Metropolitan Transit Authority, 469 U.S. 528, 105 S.Ct. 1005, 83 L.Ed.2d 1016 (1985). In response to the dissent's warnings that the Court was powerless to enforce the limitations on Congress' commerce powers because "[a]ll activities affecting commerce, even in the minutest degree, [Wickard], may be regulated and controlled by Congress," 392 U.S., at 204, 88 S.Ct., at 2028 (Douglas, J., dissenting), the Wirtz Court replied that the dissent had misread precedent as "[n]either here nor in Wickard has the Court declared that Congress may use a relatively trivial impact on commerce as an excuse for broad general regulation of state or private activities," id., at 197, n. 27, 63 S.Ct., at 89-90, n. 27. Rather, "[t]he Court has said only that where a general regulatory statute bears a substantial relation to commerce, the de minimis character of individual instances arising under that statute is of no consequence." Ibid. (first emphasis added).

Consistent with this structure, we have identified three broad categories of activity that Congress may regulate under its commerce power. Perez v. United States, supra, at 150, 91 S.Ct., at 1359; see also Hodel v. Virginia Surface Mining & Reclamation Assn., supra, at 276-277, 101 S.Ct., at 2360-2361. First, Congress may regulate the use of the channels of interstate commerce. See, e.g., Darby, 312 U.S., at 114, 61 S.Ct., at 457; Heart of Atlanta Motel, supra, at 256, 85 S.Ct., at 357 (" '[T]he authority of Congress to keep the channels of interstate commerce free from immoral and injurious uses has been frequently sustained, and is no longer open to question.' " (quoting Caminetti v. United States, 242 U.S. 470, 491, 37 S.Ct. 192, 197, 61 L.Ed. 442 (1917)). Second, Congress is empowered to regulate and protect the instrumentalities of interstate commerce, or persons or things in interstate commerce, even though the threat may come only from intrastate activities. See, e.g., Shreveport Rate Cases, 234 U.S. 342, 34 S.Ct. 833, 58 L.Ed. 1341 (1914); Southern R. Co. v. United States, 222 U.S. 20, 32 S.Ct. 2, 56 L.Ed. 72 (1911) (upholding amendments to Safety Appliance Act as applied to vehicles used in intrastate commerce); Perez, supra, at 150, 91 S.Ct., at 1359 ("[F]or example, the destruction of an aircraft (18 U.S.C. § 32), or . . . thefts from interstate shipments (18 U.S.C. § 659)"). Finally, Congress' commerce authority includes the power to regulate those activities having a substantial relation to interstate commerce, Jones & Laughlin Steel, 301 U.S., at 37, 57 S.Ct., at 624, i.e., those activities that substantially affect interstate commerce. Wirtz, supra, at 196, n. 27, 88 S.Ct., at 2024, n. 27.

Within this final category, admittedly, our case law has not been clear whether an activity must "affect" or "substantially affect" interstate commerce in order to be within Congress' power to regulate it under the Commerce Clause. Compare Preseault v. ICC, 494 U.S. 1, 17, 110 S.Ct. 914, 924-925, 108 L.Ed.2d 1 (1990), with Wirtz, supra, at 196, n. 27, 88 S.Ct., at 2024, n. 27 (the Court has never declared that "Congress may use a relatively trivial impact on commerce as an excuse for broad general regulation of state or private activities"). We conclude, consistent with the great weight of our case law, that the proper test requires an analysis of whether the regulated activity "substantially affects" interstate commerce.

We now turn to consider the power of Congress, in the light of this framework, to enact § 922(q). The first two categories of authority may be quickly disposed of: § 922(q) is not a regulation of the use of the channels of interstate commerce, nor is it an attempt to prohibit the interstate transportation of a commodity through the channels of commerce; nor can § 922(q) be justified as a regulation by which Congress has sought to protect an instrumentality of interstate commerce or a thing in interstate commerce. Thus, if § 922(q) is to be sustained, it must be under the third category as a regulation of an activity that substantially affects interstate commerce.

First, we have upheld a wide variety of congressional Acts regulating intrastate economic activity where we have concluded that the activity substantially affected interstate commerce. Examples include the regulation of intrastate coal mining; Hodel, supra, intrastate extortionate credit transactions, Perez, supra, restaurants utilizing substantial interstate supplies, McClung, supra, inns and hotels catering to interstate guests, Heart of Atlanta Motel, supra, and production and consumption of home-grown wheat, Wickard v. Filburn, 317 U.S. 111, 63 S.Ct. 82, 87 L.Ed. 122 (1942). These examples are by no means exhaustive, but the pattern is clear. Where economic activity substantially affects interstate commerce, legislation regulating that activity will be sustained.

BAN ASSAULT BANANAS

Even Wickard, which is perhaps the most far reaching example of Commerce Clause authority over intrastate activity, involved economic activity in a way that the possession of a gun in a school zone does not. Roscoe Filburn operated a small farm in Ohio, on which, in the year involved, he raised 23 acres of wheat. It was his practice to sow winter wheat in the fall, and after harvesting it in July to sell a portion of the crop, to feed part of it to poultry and livestock on the farm, to use some in making flour for home consumption, and to keep the remainder for seeding future crops. The Secretary of Agriculture assessed a penalty against him under the Agricultural Adjustment Act of 1938 because he harvested about 12 acres more wheat than his allotment under the Act permitted. The Act was designed to regulate the volume of wheat moving in interstate and foreign commerce in order to avoid surpluses and shortages, and concomitant fluctuation in wheat prices, which had previously obtained. The Court said, in an opinion sustaining the application of the Act to Filburn's activity:

"One of the primary purposes of the Act in question was to increase the market price of wheat and to that end to limit the volume thereof that could affect the market. It can hardly be denied that a factor of such volume and variability as home-consumed wheat would have a substantial influence on price and market conditions. This may arise because being in marketable condition such wheat overhangs the market and, if induced by rising prices, tends to flow into the market and check price increases. But if we assume that it is never marketed, it supplies a need of the man who grew it which would otherwise be reflected by purchases in the open market. Home-grown wheat in this sense competes with wheat in commerce." 317 U.S., at 128, 63 S.Ct., at 90-91.

Section 922(q) is a criminal statute that by its terms has nothing to do with "commerce" or any sort of economic enterprise, however broadly one might define those terms.3 Section 922(q) is not an essential part of a larger regulation of economic activity, in which the regulatory scheme could be undercut unless the intrastate activity were regulated. It cannot, therefore, be sustained under our cases upholding regulations of activities that arise out of or are connected with a commercial transaction, which viewed in the aggregate, substantially affects interstate commerce.

Second, § 922(q) contains no jurisdictional element which would ensure, through case-by-case inquiry, that the firearm possession in question affects interstate commerce. For example, in United States v. Bass, 404 U.S. 336, 92 S.Ct. 515, 30 L.Ed.2d 488 (1971), the Court interpreted former 18 U.S.C. § 1202(a), which made it a crime for a felon to "receiv[e], posses[s], or transpor[t] in commerce or affecting commerce . . . any firearm." 404 U.S., at 337, 92 S.Ct., at 517. The Court interpreted the possession component of § 1202(a) to require an additional nexus to interstate commerce both because the statute was ambiguous and because "unless Congress conveys its purpose clearly, it will not be deemed to have significantly changed the federal-state balance." Id., at 349, 92 S.Ct., at 523. The Bass Court set aside the conviction because although the Government had demonstrated that Bass had possessed a firearm, it had failed "to show the requisite nexus with interstate commerce." Id., at 347, 92 S.Ct., at 522. The Court thus interpreted the statute to reserve the constitutional question whether Congress could regulate, without more, the "mere possession" of firearms. See id., at 339, n. 4, 92 S.Ct., at 518, n. 4; see also United States v. Five Gambling Devices, 346 U.S. 441, 448, 74 S.Ct. 190, 194, 98 L.Ed. 179 (1953) (plurality opinion) ("The principle is old and deeply imbedded in our jurisprudence that this Court will construe a statute in a manner that requires decision of serious constitutional questions only if the statutory language leaves no reasonable alternative"). Unlike the statute in Bass, § 922(q) has no express jurisdictional element which might limit its reach to a discrete set of firearm possessions that additionally have an explicit connection with or effect on interstate commerce.

Although as part of our independent evaluation of constitutionality under the Commerce Clause we of course consider legislative findings, and indeed even congressional committee findings, regarding effect on interstate commerce, see, e.g., Preseault v. ICC, 494 U.S. 1, 17, 110 S.Ct. 914, 924-925, 108 L.Ed.2d 1 (1990), the Government concedes that "[n]either the statute nor its legislative history contain[s] express congressional findings regarding the effects upon interstate commerce of gun possession in a school zone." Brief for United States 5-6. We agree with the Government that Congress normally is not required to make formal findings as to the substantial burdens that an activity has on interstate commerce. See McClung, 379 U.S., at 304, 85 S.Ct., at 383-384; see also Perez, 402 U.S., at 156, 91 S.Ct., at 1362 ("Congress need [not] make particularized findings in order to legislate"). But to the extent that congressional findings would enable us to evaluate the legislative judgment that the activity in question substantially affected interstate commerce, even though no such substantial effect was visible to the naked eye, they are lacking here.4

The Government argues that Congress has accumulated institutional expertise regarding the regulation of firearms through previous enactments. Cf. Fullilove v. Klutznick, 448 U.S. 448, 503, 100 S.Ct. 2758, 2787, 65 L.Ed.2d 902 (1980) (Powell, J., concurring). We agree, however, with the Fifth Circuit that importation of previous findings to justify § 922(q) is especially inappropriate here because the "prior federal enactments or Congressional findings [do not] speak to the subject matter of section 922(q) or its relationship to interstate commerce. Indeed, section 922(q) plows thoroughly new ground and represents a sharp break with the long-standing pattern of federal firearms legislation." 2 F.3d, at 1366.

The Government's essential contention, in fine, is that we may determine here that § 922(q) is valid because possession of a firearm in a local school zone does indeed substantially affect interstate commerce. Brief for United States 17. The Government argues that possession of a firearm in a school zone may result in violent crime and that violent crime can be expected to affect the functioning of the national economy in two ways. First, the costs of violent crime are substantial, and, through the mechanism of insurance, those costs are spread throughout the population. See United States v. Evans, 928 F.2d 858, 862 (CA9 1991). Second, violent crime reduces the willingness of individuals to travel to areas within the country that are perceived to be unsafe. Cf. Heart of Atlanta Motel, 379 U.S., at 253, 85 S.Ct., at 355. The Government also argues that the presence of guns in schools poses a substantial threat to the educational process by threatening the learning environment. A handicapped educational process, in turn, will result in a less productive citizenry. That, in turn, would have an adverse effect on the Nation's economic well-being. As a result, the Government argues that Congress could rationally have concluded that § 922(q) substantially affects interstate commerce.

We pause to consider the implications of the Government's arguments. The Government admits, under its "costs of crime" reasoning, that Congress could regulate not only all violent crime, but all activities that might lead to violent crime, regardless of how tenuously they relate to interstate commerce. See Tr. of Oral Arg. 8-9. Similarly, under the Government's "national productivity" reasoning, Congress could regulate any activity that it found was related to the economic productivity of individual citizens: family law (including marriage, divorce, and child custody), for example. Under the theories that the Government presents in support of § 922(q), it is difficult to perceive any limitation on federal power, even in areas such as criminal law enforcement or education where States historically have been sovereign. Thus, if we were to accept the Government's arguments, we are hard-pressed to posit any activity by an individual that Congress is without power to regulate.

Although Justice BREYER argues that acceptance of the Government's rationales would not authorize a general federal police power, he is unable to identify any activity that the States may regulate but Congress may not. Justice BREYER posits that there might be some limitations on Congress' commerce power such as family law or certain aspects of education. Post, at __. These suggested limitations, when viewed in light of the dissent's expansive analysis, are devoid of substance.

Justice BREYER focuses, for the most part, on the threat that firearm possession in and near schools poses to the educational process and the potential economic consequences flowing from that threat. Post, at __. Specifically, the dissent reasons that (1) gun-related violence is a serious problem; (2) that problem, in turn, has an adverse effect on classroom learning; and (3) that adverse effect on classroom learning, in turn, represents a substantial threat to trade and commerce. Post, at ____. This analysis would be equally applicable, if not more so, to subjects such as family law and direct regulation of education.

For instance, if Congress can, pursuant to its Commerce Clause power, regulate activities that adversely affect the learning environment, then, a fortiori, it also can regulate the educational process directly. Congress could determine that a school's curriculum has a "significant" effect on the extent of classroom learning. As a result, Congress could mandate a federal curriculum for local elementary and secondary schools because what is taught in local schools has a significant "effect on classroom learning," cf. post, at __, and that, in turn, has a substantial effect on interstate commerce.

Justice BREYER rejects our reading of precedent and argues that "Congress . . . could rationally conclude that schools fall on the commercial side of the line." Post, at ___. Again, Justice BREYER's rationale lacks any real limits because, depending on the level of generality, any activity can be looked upon as commercial. Under the dissent's rationale, Congress could just as easily look at child rearing as "fall[ing] on the commercial side of the line" because it provides a "valuable service—namely, to equip [children] with the skills they need to survive in life and, more specifically, in the workplace." Ibid. We do not doubt that Congress has authority under the Commerce Clause to regulate numerous commercial activities that substantially affect interstate commerce and also affect the educational process. That authority, though broad, does not include the authority to regulate each and every aspect of local schools.

Admittedly, a determination whether an intrastate activity is commercial or noncommercial may in some cases result in legal uncertainty. But, so long as Congress' authority is limited to those powers enumerated in the Constitution, and so long as those enumerated powers are interpreted as having judicially enforceable outer limits, congressional legislation under the Commerce Clause always will engender "legal uncertainty." Post, at ___. As Chief Justice Marshall stated in McCulloch v. Maryland, 4 Wheat. 316, 4 L.Ed. 579 (1819):

> "The [federal] government is acknowledged by all to be one of enumerated powers. The principle, that it can exercise only the powers granted to it . . . is now universally admitted. But the question respect ing the extent of the powers actually granted, is perpetually arising, and will

probably continue to arise, as long as our system shall exist." Id., at 405.

See also Gibbons v. Ogden, 9 Wheat., at 195 ("The enumeration presupposes something not enumerated"). The Constitution mandates this uncertainty by withholding from Congress a plenary police power that would authorize enactment of every type of legislation. See U.S. Const., Art. I, § 8. Congress has operated within this framework of legal uncertainty ever since this Court determined that it was the judiciary's duty "to say what the law is." Marbury v. Madison, 1 Cranch. 137, 177, 2 L.Ed. 60 (1803) (Marshall, C.J.). Any possible benefit from eliminating this "legal uncertainty" would be at the expense of the Constitution's system of enumerated powers.

In Jones & Laughlin Steel, 301 U.S., at 37, 57 S.Ct., at 624, we held that the question of congressional power under the Commerce Clause "is necessarily one of degree." To the same effect is the concurring opinion of Justice Cardozo in Schecter Poultry:

"There is a view of causation that would obliterate the distinction of what is national and what is local in the activities of commerce. Motion at the outer rim is communicated perceptibly, though minutely, to recording instruments at the center. A society such as ours 'is an elastic medium which transmits all tremors throughout its territory; the only question is of their size.' " 295 U.S., at 554, 55 S.Ct., at 853 (quoting United States v. A.L.A. Schecter Poultry Corp., 76 F.2d 617, 624 (CA2 1935) (L. Hand, J., concurring)).

These are not precise formulations, and in the nature of things they cannot be. But we think they point the way to a correct decision of this case. The possession of a gun in a local school zone is in no sense an economic activity that might, through repetition elsewhere, substantially affect any sort of interstate commerce. Respondent was a local student at a local school; there is no indication that he had recently moved in interstate commerce, and there is no requirement that his possession of the firearm have any concrete tie to interstate commerce.

To uphold the Government's contentions here, we would have to pile inference upon inference in a manner that would bid fair to convert congressional authority under the Commerce Clause to a general police power of the sort retained by the States. Admittedly, some of our prior cases have taken long steps down that road, giving great deference to congressional action. See supra, at ____. The broad language in these opinions has suggested the possibility of additional expansion, but we decline here to proceed any further. To do so would require us to conclude that the Constitution's enumeration of powers does not presuppose something not enumerated, cf. Gibbons v. Ogden, supra, at 195, and that there never will be a distinction between what is truly national and what is truly local, cf. Jones & Laughlin Steel, supra, at 30, 57 S.Ct., at 621. This we are unwilling to do.

For the foregoing reasons the judgment of the Court of Appeals is

Affirmed.

Justice KENNEDY, with whom Justice O'CONNOR joins, concurring.

BAN ASSAULT BANANAS

The history of the judicial struggle to interpret the Commerce Clause during the transition from the economic system the Founders knew to the single, national market still emergent in our own era counsels great restraint before the Court determines that the Clause is insufficient to support an exercise of the national power. That history gives me some pause about today's decision, but I join the Court's opinion with these observations on what I conceive to be its necessary though limited holding.

Chief Justice Marshall announced that the national authority reaches "that commerce which concerns more States than one" and that the commerce power "is complete in itself, may be exercised to its utmost extent, and acknowledges no limitations, other than are prescribed in the constitution." Gibbons v. Ogden, 9 Wheat. 1, 194, 196, 6 L.Ed. 23 (1824). His statements can be understood now as an early and authoritative recognition that the Commerce Clause grants Congress extensive power and ample discretion to determine its appropriate exercise. The progression of our Commerce Clause cases from Gibbons to the present was not marked, however, by a coherent or consistent course of interpretation; for neither the course of technological advance nor the foundational principles for the jurisprudence itself were self-evident to the courts that sought to resolve contemporary disputes by enduring principles.

Furthermore, for almost a century after the adoption of the Constitution, the Court's Commerce Clause decisions did not concern the authority of Congress to legislate.

Rather, the Court faced the related but quite distinct question of the authority of the States to regulate matters that would be within the commerce power had Congress chosen to act. The simple fact was that in the early years of the Republic, Congress seldom perceived the necessity to exercise its power in circumstances where its authority would be called into question. The Court's initial task, therefore, was to elaborate the theories that would permit the States to act where Congress had not done so. Not the least part of the problem was the unresolved question whether the congressional power was exclusive, a question reserved by Chief Justice Marshall in Gibbons v. Ogden, supra, at 209-210.

At the midpoint of the 19th century, the Court embraced the principle that the States and the National Government both have authority to regulate certain matters absent the congressional determination to displace local law or the necessity for the Court to invalidate local law because of the dormant national power. Cooley v. Board of Wardens of Port of Philadelphia, 12 How. 299, 318-321, 13 L.Ed. 996 (1852). But the utility of that solution was not at once apparent, see generally F. Frankfurter, The Commerce Clause under Marshall, Taney and Waite (1937) (hereinafter Frankfurter), and difficulties of application persisted, see Leisy v. Hardin, 135 U.S. 100, 122-125, 10 S.Ct. 681, 688-690, 34 L.Ed. 128 (1890).

One approach the Court used to inquire into the lawfulness of state authority was to draw content-based or subject-matter distinctions, thus defining by semantic or formalistic categories those activities that were commerce and those that were not. For instance, in deciding that a State could prohibit the in-state manufacture of liquor intended for out-of-state shipment, it distinguished between manufacture and commerce. "No distinction is more popular to the common mind, or more clearly expressed in economic and political literature, than that between manufactur[e] and commerce. Manufacture is transformation—the fashioning of raw materials into a change of form for use. The functions of commerce are different." Kidd v. Pearson, 128 U.S. 1, 20, 9 S.Ct. 6, 10, 32 L.Ed. 346 (1888). Though that approach likely would not have survived even if confined to the question of a State's authority to enact legislation, it was not at all propitious when applied to the quite different question of what subjects were within the reach of the national power when Congress chose to exercise it.

This became evident when the Court began to confront federal economic regulation enacted in response to the rapid industrial development in the late 19th century. Thus, it relied upon the manufacture-commerce dichotomy in United States v. E.C. Knight Co., 156 U.S. 1, 15 S.Ct. 249, 39 L.Ed. 325 (1895), where a manufacturers' combination controlling some 98% of the Nation's domestic sugar refining capacity was held to be outside the reach of the Sherman Act. Conspiracies to control manufacture, agriculture, mining, production, wages, or prices, the Court explained, had too "indirect" an effect on interstate commerce. Id., at 16, 15 S.Ct., at 255. And in Adair v. United States, 208 U.S. 161, 28 S.Ct. 277, 52 L.Ed. 436 (1908), the

Court rejected the view that the commerce power might extend to activities that, although local in the sense of having originated within a single state, nevertheless had a practical effect on interstate commercial activity. The Court concluded that there was not a "legal or logical connection . . . between an employe's membership in a labor organization and the carrying on of interstate commerce," id., at 178, 28 S.Ct., at 282, and struck down a federal statute forbidding the discharge of an employee because of his membership in a labor organization. See also The Employers' Liability Cases, 207 U.S. 463, 497, 28 S.Ct. 141, 145, 52 L.Ed. 297 (1908) (invalidating statute creating negligence action against common carriers for personal injuries of employees sustained in the course of employment, because the statute "regulates the persons because they engage in interstate commerce and does not alone regulate the business of interstate commerce").

Even before the Court committed itself to sustaining federal legislation on broad principles of economic practicality, it found it necessary to depart from these decisions. The Court disavowed E.C. Knight's reliance on the manufacturing-commerce distinction in Standard Oil Co. of New Jersey v. United States, 221 U.S. 1, 68-69, 31 S.Ct. 502, 518-519, 55 L.Ed. 619 (1911), declaring that approach "unsound." The Court likewise rejected the rationale of Adair when it decided, in Texas & New Orleans R. Co. v. Railway Clerks, 281 U.S. 548, 570-571, 50 S.Ct. 427, 433-434, 74 L.Ed. 1034 (1930), that Congress had the power to regulate matters pertaining to the organization of railroad workers.

In another line of cases, the Court addressed Congress' efforts to impede local activities it considered undesirable by prohibiting the interstate movement of some essential element. In the Lottery Case, 188 U.S. 321, 23 S.Ct. 321, 47 L.Ed. 492 (1903), the Court rejected the argument that Congress lacked power to prohibit the interstate movement of lottery tickets because it had power only to regulate, not to prohibit. See also Hipolite Egg Co. v. United States, 220 U.S. 45, 31 S.Ct. 364, 55 L.Ed. 364 (1911); Hoke v. United States, 227 U.S. 308, 33 S.Ct. 281, 57 L.Ed. 523 (1913). In Hammer v. Dagenhart, 247 U.S. 251, 38 S.Ct. 529, 62 L.Ed. 1101 (1918), however, the Court insisted that the power to regulate commerce "is directly the contrary of the assumed right to forbid commerce from moving," id., at 269-270, 38 S.Ct., at 530, and struck down a prohibition on the interstate transportation of goods manufactured in violation of child labor laws.

Even while it was experiencing difficulties in finding satisfactory principles in these cases, the Court was pursuing a more sustainable and practical approach in other lines of decisions, particularly those involving the regulation of railroad rates. In the Minnesota Rate Cases, 230 U.S. 352, 33 S.Ct. 729, 57 L.Ed. 1511 (1913), the Court upheld a state rate order, but observed that Congress might be empowered to regulate in this area if "by reason of the interblending of the interstate and intrastate operations of interstate carriers" the regulation of interstate rates could not be maintained without restrictions on "intrastate rates which substantially affect the former." Id., at 432-433, 33 S.Ct., at 753-754. And in the Shreveport Rate Cases, 234

U.S. 342, 34 S.Ct. 833, 58 L.Ed. 1341 (1914), the Court upheld an ICC order fixing railroad rates with the explanation that congressional authority, "extending to these interstate carriers as instruments of interstate commerce, necessarily embraces the right to control their operations in all matters having such a close and substantial relation to interstate traffic that the control is essential or appropriate to the security of that traffic, to the efficiency of the interstate service, and to the maintenance of conditions under which interstate commerce may be conducted upon fair terms and without molestation or hindrance." Id., at 351, 34 S.Ct., at 836.

Even the most confined interpretation of "commerce" would embrace transportation between the States, so the rate cases posed much less difficulty for the Court than cases involving manufacture or production. Nevertheless, the Court's recognition of the importance of a practical conception of the commerce power was not altogether confined to the rate cases. In Swift & Co. v. United States, 196 U.S. 375, 25 S.Ct. 276, 49 L.Ed. 518 (1905), the Court upheld the application of federal antitrust law to a combination of meat dealers that occurred in one State but that restrained trade in cattle "sent for sale from a place in one State, with the expectation that they will end their transit . . . in another." Id., at 398, 25 S.Ct., at 280. The Court explained that "commerce among the States is not a technical legal conception, but a practical one, drawn from the course of business." Id., at 398, 25 S.Ct., at 280. Chief Justice Taft followed the same approach in upholding federal regulation of stockyards in Stafford v. Wallace, 258

U.S. 495, 42 S.Ct. 397, 66 L.Ed. 735 (1922). Speaking for the Court, he rejected a "nice and technical inquiry," id., at 519, 42 S.Ct., at 403, when the local transactions at issue could not "be separated from the movement to which they contribute," id., at 516, 42 S.Ct., at 402.

Reluctance of the Court to adopt that approach in all of its cases caused inconsistencies in doctrine to persist, however. In addressing New Deal legislation the Court resuscitated the abandoned abstract distinction between direct and indirect effects on interstate commerce. See Carter v. Carter Coal Co., 298 U.S. 238, 309, 56 S.Ct. 855, 872, 80 L.Ed. 1160 (1936) (Act regulating price of coal and wages and hours for miners held to have only "secondary and indirect" effect on interstate commerce); Railroad Retirement Bd. v. Alton R. Co., 295 U.S. 330, 368, 55 S.Ct. 758, 771, 79 L.Ed. 1468 (1935) (compulsory retirement and pension plan for railroad carrier employees too "remote from any regulation of commerce as such"); A.L.A. Schechter Poultry Corp. v. United States, 295 U.S. 495, 548, 55 S.Ct. 837, 851, 79 L.Ed. 1570 (1935) (wage and hour law provision of National Industrial Recovery Act had "no direct relation to interstate commerce").

The case that seems to mark the Court's definitive commitment to the practical conception of the commerce power is NLRB v. Jones & Laughlin Steel Corp., 301 U.S. 1, 57 S.Ct. 615, 81 L.Ed. 893 (1937), where the Court sustained labor laws that applied to manufacturing facilities, making no real attempt to distinguish Carter, supra, and Schechter, supra. 301 U.S., at 40-41, 57 S.Ct., at 625-626. The deference given to Congress has since been confirmed. United States v. Darby, 312 U.S. 100, 116-117, 61 S.Ct. 451, 458-459, 85 L.Ed. 609 (1941), overruled Hammer v. Dagenhart, supra. And in Wickard v. Filburn, 317 U.S. 111, 63 S.Ct. 82, 87 L.Ed. 122 (1942), the Court disapproved E.C. Knight and the entire line of direct-indirect and manufacture-production cases, explaining that "broader interpretations of the Commerce Clause [were] destined to supersede the earlier ones," id., at 122, 63 S.Ct., at 88, and "whatever terminology is used, the criterion is necessarily one of degree and must be so defined. This does not satisfy those who seek mathematical or rigid formulas. But such formulas are not provided by the great concepts of the Constitution," id., at 123, n. 24, 63 S.Ct., at 88, n. 24. Later examples of the exercise of federal power where commercial transactions were the subject of regulation include Heart of Atlanta Motel, Inc. v. United States, 379 U.S. 241, 85 S.Ct. 348, 13 L.Ed.2d 258 (1964), Katzenbach v. McClung, 379 U.S. 294, 85 S.Ct. 377, 13 L.Ed.2d 290 (1964), and Perez v. United States, 402 U.S. 146, 91 S.Ct. 1357, 28 L.Ed.2d 686 (1971). These and like authorities are within the fair ambit of the Court's practical conception of commercial regulation and are not called in question by our decision today.

The history of our Commerce Clause decisions contains at least two lessons of relevance to this case. The first, as stated at the outset, is the imprecision of content-based boundaries used without more to define the limits of the Commerce Clause. The second, related to the first but of even greater consequence, is that the Court as an institution and the legal system as a whole have an immense stake in the stability of our Commerce Clause jurisprudence as it has evolved to this point. Stare decisis operates with great force in counseling us not to call in question the essential principles now in place respecting the congressional power to regulate transactions of a commercial nature. That fundamental restraint on our power forecloses us from reverting to an understanding of commerce that would serve only an 18th-century economy, dependent then upon production and trading practices that had changed but little over the preceding centuries; it also mandates against returning to the time when congressional authority to regulate undoubted commercial activities was limited by a judicial determination that those matters had an insufficient connection to an interstate system. Congress can regulate in the commercial sphere on the assumption that we have a single market and a unified purpose to build a stable national economy.

In referring to the whole subject of the federal and state balance, we said this just three Terms ago:

"This framework has been sufficiently flexible over the past two centuries to allow for enormous changes in the nature of government. The Federal Government undertakes activities today that would have been unimaginable to the Framers in two senses: first, because the Framers would not have conceived that any government would conduct such activities; and second, because the Framers would not have believed that the Federal Government, rather than the States, would assume such responsibilities. Yet the powers conferred upon the Federal Government by the Constitution were phrased in language broad enough to allow for the expansion of the Federal Government's role." New York v. United States, 505 U.S. ----, ----, 112 S.Ct. 2408, 2418, 120 L.Ed.2d 120 (1992) (emphasis omitted).

It does not follow, however, that in every instance the Court lacks the authority and responsibility to review congressional attempts to alter the federal balance. This case requires us to consider our place in the design of the Government and to appreciate the significance of federalism in the whole structure of the Constitution.

Of the various structural elements in the Constitution, separation of powers, checks and balances, judicial review, and federalism, only concerning the last does there seem to be much uncertainty respecting the existence, and the content, of standards that allow the judiciary to play a significant role in maintaining the design contemplated by the Framers. Although the resolution of specific cases has proved difficult, we have derived from the Constitution workable standards to assist in preserving separation of powers and checks and balances. See, e.g., Prize Cases, 2 Black 635, 17 L.Ed. 459 (1863); Youngstown Sheet & Tube Co. v. Sawyer, 343 U.S. 579, 72 S.Ct. 863, 96 L.Ed. 1153 (1952); United States v. Nixon, 418 U.S. 683, 94 S.Ct. 3090, 41 L.Ed.2d 1039 (1974); Buckley v. Valeo, 424 U.S. 1, 96 S.Ct. 612, 46 L.Ed.2d 659 (1976); INS v. Chadha, 462 U.S. 919, 103 S.Ct. 2764, 77 L.Ed.2d 317 (1983); Bowsher v. Synar, 478 U.S. 714, 106 S.Ct. 3181, 92 L.Ed.2d 583 (1986); Plaut v. Spendthrift Farm, --- U.S. ----, 115 S.Ct. 1447, ---

L.Ed.2d ---- (1995). These standards are by now well accepted. Judicial review is also established beyond question, Marbury v. Madison, 1 Cranch 137, 2 L.Ed. 60 (1803), and though we may differ when applying its principles, see, e.g., Planned Parenthood of Southeastern Pennsylvania v. Casey, 505 U.S. ----, 112 S.Ct. 2791, 120 L.Ed.2d 674 (1992), its legitimacy is undoubted. Our role in preserving the federal balance seems more tenuous.

There is irony in this, because of the four structural elements in the Constitution just mentioned, federalism was the unique contribution of the Framers to political science and political theory. See Friendly, Federalism: A Forward, 86 Yale L.J. 1019 (1977); G. Wood, The Creation of the American Republic, 1776-1787, pp. 524-532, 564 (1969). Though on the surface the idea may seem counterintuitive, it was the insight of the Framers that freedom was enhanced by the creation of two governments, not one. "In the compound republic of America, the power surrendered by the people is first divided between two distinct governments, and then the portion allotted to each subdivided among distinct and separate departments. Hence a double security arises to the rights of the people. The different governments will control each other, at the same time that each will be controlled by itself." The Federalist No. 51, p. 323 (C. Rossiter ed. 1961) (J. Madison). See also Gregory v. Ashcroft, 501 U.S. 452, 458-459, 111 S.Ct. 2395, 2400, 115 L.Ed.2d 410 (1991) ("Just as the separation and independence of the coordinate branches of the Federal Government serve to prevent the accumulation of excessive power in any one branch, a healthy balance of power between the States and the Federal Government will reduce the risk of tyranny and abuse from either front. . . . In the tension between federal and state power lies the promise of liberty"); New York v. United States, supra, at ----, 112 S.Ct., at 2431 ("[T]he Constitution divides authority between federal and state governments for the protection of individuals. State sovereignty is not just an end in itself: 'Rather, federalism secures to citizens the liberties that derive from the diffusion of sovereign power' ") (quoting Coleman v. Thompson, 501 U.S. 722, 759, 111 S.Ct. 2546, 2570, 115 L.Ed.2d 640 (1991) (Blackmun, J., dissenting)).

The theory that two governments accord more liberty than one requires for its realization two distinct and discernable lines of political accountability: one between the citizens and the Federal Government; the second between the citizens and the States. If, as Madison expected, the federal and state governments are to control each other, see The Federalist No. 51, and hold each other in check by competing for the affections of the people, see The Federalist No. 46, those citizens must have some means of knowing which of the two governments to hold accountable for the failure to perform a given function. "Federalism serves to assign political responsibility, not to obscure it." FTC v. Ticor Title Ins. Co., 504 U.S. 621, 636, 112 S.Ct. 2169, 2178, 119 L.Ed.2d 410 (1992). Were the Federal Government to take over the regulation of entire areas of traditional state concern, areas having nothing to do with the regulation of commercial activities, the boundaries between the spheres of federal and state authority would blur and political responsibility would become illusory. See New York v. United States, supra, at ----, 112 S.Ct., at 2417-2422; FERC v. Mississippi, 456 U.S. 742, 787, 102 S.Ct. 2126, 2152, 72 L.Ed.2d 532 (1982) (O'CONNOR, J., concurring in judgment in part and dissenting in part). The resultant inability to hold either branch of the government answerable to the citizens is more dangerous even than devolving too much authority to the remote central power.

To be sure, one conclusion that could be drawn from The Federalist Papers is that the balance between national and state power is entrusted in its entirety to the political process. Madison's observation that "the people ought not surely to be precluded from giving most of their confidence where they may discover it to be most due," The Federalist No. 46, p. 295 (C. Rossiter ed. 1961), can be interpreted to say that the essence of responsibility for a shift in power from the State to the Federal Government rests upon a political judgment, though he added assurance that "the State governments could have little to apprehend, because it is only within a certain sphere that the federal power can, in the nature of things, be advantageously administered," ibid. Whatever the judicial role, it is axiomatic that Congress does have substantial discretion and control over the federal balance.

For these reasons, it would be mistaken and mischievous for the political branches to forget that the sworn obligation to preserve and protect the Constitution in maintaining the federal balance is their own in the first and primary instance. In the Webster-Hayne Debates, see

The Great Speeches and Orations of Daniel Webster 227-272 (E. Whipple ed. 1879), and the debates over the Civil Rights Acts, see Hearings on S. 1732 before the Senate Committee on Commerce, 88th Cong., 1st Sess., pts. 1-3 (1963), some Congresses have accepted responsibility to confront the great questions of the proper federal balance in terms of lasting consequences for the constitutional design. The political branches of the Government must fulfill this grave constitutional obligation if democratic liberty and the federalism that secures it are to endure.

At the same time, the absence of structural mechanisms to require those officials to undertake this principled task, and the momentary political convenience often attendant upon their failure to do so, argue against a complete renunciation of the judicial role. Although it is the obligation of all officers of the Government to respect the constitutional design, see Public Citizen v. Department of Justice, 491 U.S. 440, 466, 109 S.Ct. 2558, 2572-2573, 105 L.Ed.2d 377 (1989); Rostker v. Goldberg, 453 U.S. 57, 64, 101 S.Ct. 2646, 2651, 69 L.Ed.2d 478 (1981), the federal balance is too essential a part of our constitutional structure and plays too vital a role in securing freedom for us to admit inability to intervene when one or the other level of Government has tipped the scales too far.

In the past this Court has participated in maintaining the federal balance through judicial exposition of doctrines such as abstention, see, e.g., Younger v. Harris, 401 U.S. 37, 91 S.Ct. 746, 27 L.Ed.2d 669 (1971); Railroad Comm'n of Texas v. Pullman Co., 312 U.S. 496, 61 S.Ct. 643, 85 L.Ed.

971 (1941); Burford v. Sun Oil Co., 319 U.S. 315, 63 S.Ct. 1098, 87 L.Ed. 1424 (1943), the rules for determining the primacy of state law, see, e.g., Erie R. Co. v. Tompkins, 304 U.S. 64, 58 S.Ct. 817, 82 L.Ed. 1188 (1938), the doctrine of adequate and independent state grounds, see, e.g., Murdock v. City of Memphis, 87 U.S. 590, 22 L.Ed. 429 (1875); Michigan v. Long, 463 U.S. 1032, 103 S.Ct. 3469, 77 L.Ed.2d 1201 (1983), the whole jurisprudence of preemption, see, e.g., Rice v. Santa Fe Elevator Corp., 331 U.S. 218, 67 S.Ct. 1146, 91 L.Ed. 1447 (1947); Cipollone v. Liggett Group, Inc., 505 U.S. ----, 112 S.Ct. 2608, 120 L.Ed.2d 407 (1992), and many of the rules governing our habeas jurisprudence, see, e.g., Coleman v. Thompson, supra; McCleskey v. Zant, 499 U.S. 467, 111 S.Ct. 1454, 113 L.Ed.2d 517 (1991); Teague v. Lane, 489 U.S. 288, 109 S.Ct. 1060, 103 L.Ed.2d 334 (1989); Rose v. Lundy, 455 U.S. 509, 102 S.Ct. 1198, 71 L.Ed.2d 379 (1982); Wainwright v. Sykes, 433 U.S. 72, 97 S.Ct. 2497, 53 L.Ed.2d 594 (1977).

Our ability to preserve this principle under the Commerce Clause has presented a much greater challenge. See supra, at ____-____. "This clause has throughout the Court's history been the chief source of its adjudications regarding federalism," and "no other body of opinions affords a fairer or more revealing test of judicial qualities." Frankfurter 66-67. But as the branch whose distinctive duty it is to declare "what the law is," Marbury v. Madison, 1 Cranch, at 177, we are often called upon to resolve questions of constitutional law not susceptible to the mechanical application of bright and clear lines. The substantial element of political judgment in Commerce

Clause matters leaves our institutional capacity to intervene more in doubt than when we decide cases, for instance, under the Bill of Rights even though clear and bright lines are often absent in the latter class of disputes. See County of Allegheny v. American Civil Liberties Union, Greater Pittsburgh Chapter, 492 U.S. 573, 630, 109 S.Ct. 3086, 3120, 106 L.Ed.2d 472 (1989) (O'CONNOR, J., concurring in part and concurring in judgment) ("We cannot avoid the obligation to draw lines, often close and difficult lines" in adjudicating constitutional rights). But our cases do not teach that we have no role at all in determining the meaning of the Commerce Clause.

Our position in enforcing the dormant Commerce Clause is instructive. The Court's doctrinal approach in that area has likewise "taken some turns." Oklahoma Tax Comm'n v. Jefferson Lines, Inc., 514 U.S. ----, ----, 115 S.Ct. 1331, 1336, --- L.Ed.2d ---- (1995). Yet in contrast to the prevailing skepticism that surrounds our ability to give meaning to the explicit text of the Commerce Clause, there is widespread acceptance of our authority to enforce the dormant Commerce Clause, which we have but inferred from the constitutional structure as a limitation on the power of the States. One element of our dormant Commerce Clause jurisprudence has been the principle that the States may not impose regulations that place an undue burden on interstate commerce, even where those regulations do not discriminate between in-state and out-of-state businesses. See Brown-Forman Distillers Corp. v. New York State Liquor Authority, 476 U.S. 573, 579, 106 S.Ct. 2080, 2084, 90 L.Ed.2d 552 (1986) (citing Pike v. Bruce

Church, Inc., 397 U.S. 137, 142, 90 S.Ct. 844, 847, 25 L.Ed.2d 174 (1970)). Distinguishing between regulations that do place an undue burden on interstate commerce and regulations that do not depends upon delicate judgments. True, if we invalidate a state law, Congress can in effect overturn our judgment, whereas in a case announcing that Congress has transgressed its authority, the decision is more consequential, for it stands unless Congress can revise its law to demonstrate its commercial character. This difference no doubt informs the circumspection with which we invalidate an Act of Congress, but it does not mitigate our duty to recognize meaningful limits on the commerce power of Congress.

The statute before us upsets the federal balance to a degree that renders it an unconstitutional assertion of the commerce power, and our intervention is required. As THE CHIEF JUSTICE explains, unlike the earlier cases to come before the Court here neither the actors nor their conduct have a commercial character, and neither the purposes nor the design of the statute have an evident commercial nexus. See ante, at ____-____. The statute makes the simple possession of a gun within 1,000 feet of the grounds of the school a criminal offense. In a sense any conduct in this interdependent world of ours has an ultimate commercial origin or consequence, but we have not yet said the commerce power may reach so far. If Congress attempts that extension, then at the least we must inquire whether the exercise of national power seeks to intrude upon an area of traditional state concern.

An interference of these dimensions occurs here, for it is well established that education is a traditional concern of the States. Milliken v. Bradley, 418 U.S. 717, 741-742, 94 S.Ct. 3112, 3125-3126, 41 L.Ed.2d 1069 (1974); Epperson v. Arkansas, 393 U.S. 97, 104, 89 S.Ct. 266, 270, 21 L.Ed.2d 228 (1968). The proximity to schools, including of course schools owned and operated by the States or their subdivisions, is the very premise for making the conduct criminal. In these circumstances, we have a particular duty to insure that the federal-state balance is not destroyed. Cf. Rice, supra, at 230, 67 S.Ct., at 1152 ("[W]e start with the assumption that the historic police powers of the States" are not displaced by a federal statute "unless that was the clear and manifest purpose of Congress"); Florida Lime & Avocado Growers, Inc. v. Paul, 373 U.S. 132, 146, 83 S.Ct. 1210, 1219, 10 L.Ed.2d 248 (1963).

While it is doubtful that any State, or indeed any reasonable person, would argue that it is wise policy to allow students to carry guns on school premises, considerable disagreement exists about how best to accomplish that goal. In this circumstance, the theory and utility of our federalism are revealed, for the States may perform their role as laboratories for experimentation to devise various solutions where the best solution is far from clear. See San Antonio Independent School Dist. v. Rodriguez, 411 U.S. 1, 49-50, 93 S.Ct. 1278, 1304-05, 36 L.Ed.2d 16 (1973); New State Ice Co. v. Liebmann, 285 U.S. 262, 311, 52 S.Ct. 371, 386-87, 76 L.Ed. 747 (1932) (Brandeis, J., dissenting)).

BAN ASSAULT BANANAS

If a State or municipality determines that harsh criminal sanctions are necessary and wise to deter students from carrying guns on school premises, the reserved powers of the States are sufficient to enact those measures. Indeed, over 40 States already have criminal laws outlawing the possession of firearms on or near school grounds. See, e.g., Alaska Stat.Ann. §§ 11.61.195(a)(2)(A), 11.61.220(a)(4)(A) (Supp.1994); Cal.Penal Code Ann. § 626.9 (West Supp.1994); Mass.Gen.Laws c. 269, § 10(j) (1992); N.J.Stat.Ann. § 2C:39-5(e) (West Supp.1994); Va.Code Ann. § 18.2-308.1 (1988); Wis.Stat. § 948.605 (1991-1992).

Other, more practicable means to rid the schools of guns may be thought by the citizens of some States to be preferable for the safety and welfare of the schools those States are charged with maintaining. See Brief for National Conference of State Legislatures et al., as Amici Curiae 26-30 (injection of federal officials into local problems causes friction and diminishes political accountability of state and local governments). These might include inducements to inform on violators where the information leads to arrests or confiscation of the guns, see C. Lima, Schools May Launch Weapons Hot Line, L.A. Times, Jan. 13, 1995, part B, p. 1, col. 5; Reward for Tips on Guns in Tucson Schools, The Arizona Republic, Jan. 7, 1995, p. B2; programs to encourage the voluntary surrender of guns with some provision for amnesty, see A. Zaidan, Akron Rallies to Save Youths, The Plain Dealer, Mar. 2, 1995, p. 1B; M. Swift, Legislators Consider Plan to Get Guns Off Streets, Hartford Courant, Apr. 29, 1992, p. A4; penalties imposed on parents or guardians for failure to supervise the child, see, e.g.,

Okla.Stat., Tit. 21, § 858 (Supp.1995) (fining parents who allow students to possess firearm at school); Tenn.Code Ann. § 39-17-1312 (Supp.1992) (misdemeanor for parents to allow student to possess firearm at school); Straight Shooter: Gov. Casey's Reasonable Plan to Control Assault Weapons, Pittsburgh Post-Gazette, Mar. 14, 1994, p. B2 (proposed bill); E. Bailey, Anti-Crime Measures Top Legislators' Agenda, L.A. Times, Mar. 7, 1994, part B, p. 1, col. 2 (same); G. Krupa, New Gun-Control Plans Could Tighten Local Law, The Boston Globe, June 20, 1993, p. 29; laws providing for suspension or expulsion of gun-toting students, see, e.g., Ala.Code § 16-1-24.1 (Supp.1994); Ind.Code § 20-8.1-5-4(b)(1)(D) (1993); Ky.Rev.Stat.Ann. § 158.150(1)(a) (Michie 1992); Wash.Rev.Code § 9.41.280 (1994), or programs for expulsion with assignment to special facilities, see J. Martin, Legislators Poised to Take Harsher Stand on Guns in Schools, The Seattle Times, Feb. 1, 1995, p. B1 (automatic-year-long expulsion for students with guns and intense semester-long reentry program).

The statute now before us forecloses the States from experimenting and exercising their own judgment in an area to which States lay claim by right of history and expertise, and it does so by regulating an activity beyond the realm of commerce in the ordinary and usual sense of that term. The tendency of this statute to displace state regulation in areas of traditional state concern is evident from its territorial operation. There are over 100,000 elementary and secondary schools in the United States. See U.S. Dept. of Education, National Center for Education Statistics, Digest of Education Statistics 73, 104 (NCES

94-115, 1994) (Tables 63, 94). Each of these now has an invisible federal zone extending 1,000 feet beyond the (often irregular) boundaries of the school property. In some communities no doubt it would be difficult to navigate without infringing on those zones. Yet throughout these areas, school officials would find their own programs for the prohibition of guns in danger of displacement by the federal authority unless the State chooses to enact a parallel rule.

This is not a case where the etiquette of federalism has been violated by a formal command from the National Government directing the State to enact a certain policy, cf. New York v. United States, 505 U.S. ----, 112 S.Ct. 2408, 120 L.Ed.2d 120 (1992), or to organize its governmental functions in a certain way, cf. FERC v. Mississippi, 456 U.S., at 781, 102 S.Ct., at 2149 (O'CONNOR, J., concurring in judgment in part and dissenting in part). While the intrusion on state sovereignty may not be as severe in this instance as in some of our recent Tenth Amendment cases, the intrusion is nonetheless significant. Absent a stronger connection or identification with commercial concerns that are central to the Commerce Clause, that interference contradicts the federal balance the Framers designed and that this Court is obliged to enforce.

For these reasons, I join in the opinion and judgment of the Court. djQ Justice THOMAS, concurring.

The Court today properly concludes that the Commerce Clause does not grant Congress the authority to prohibit gun possession within 1,000 feet of a school, as it attempted to do in the Gun-Free School Zones Act of 1990, Pub.L. 101-647, 104 Stat. 4844. Although I join the majority, I write separately to observe that our case law has drifted far from the original understanding of the Commerce Clause. In a future case, we ought to temper our Commerce Clause jurisprudence in a manner that both makes sense of our more recent case law and is more faithful to the original understanding of that Clause.

We have said that Congress may regulate not only "Commerce . . . among the several states," U.S. Const., Art. I, § 8, cl. 3, but also anything that has a "substantial effect" on such commerce. This test, if taken to its logical extreme, would give Congress a "police power" over all aspects of American life. Unfortunately, we have never come to grips with this implication of our substantial effects formula. Although we have supposedly applied the substantial effects test for the past 60 years, we always have rejected readings of the Commerce Clause and the scope of federal power that would permit Congress to exercise a police power; our cases are quite clear that there are real limits to federal power. See New York v. United States, 505 U.S. ----, ----, 112 S.Ct. 2408, 2417, 120 L.Ed.2d 120 (1992) ("[N]o one disputes the proposition that '[t]he Constitution created a Federal Government of limited powers' ") (quoting Gregory v. Ashcroft, 501 U.S. 452, 457, 111 S.Ct. 2395, 2399, 115 L.Ed.2d 410 (1991); Maryland v. Wirtz, 392 U.S. 183, 196, 88 S.Ct. 2017, 2023-24, 20 L.Ed.2d 1020 (1968); NLRB v. Jones & Laughlin Steel Corp., 301 U.S. 1, 37, 57 S.Ct. 615, 624, 81 L.Ed. 893 (1937). Cf. Chisholm v. Georgia, 2 Dall. 419, 435, 1

L.Ed. 440 (1793) (Iredell, J.) ("Each State in the Union is sovereign as to all the powers reserved. It must necessarily be so, because the United States have no claim to any authority but such as the States have surrendered to them"). Indeed, on this crucial point, the majority and Justice BREYER agree in principle: the Federal Government has nothing approaching a police power. Compare ante, at ____-____ with post, at __, the sweeping nature of our current test enables the dissent to argue that Congress can regulate gun possession. But it seems to me that the power to regulate "commerce" can by no means encompass authority over mere gun possession, any more than it empowers the Federal Government to regulate marriage, littering, or cruelty to animals, throughout the 50 States. Our Constitution quite properly leaves such matters to the individual States, notwithstanding these activities' effects on interstate commerce. Any interpretation of the Commerce Clause that even suggests that Congress could regulate such matters is in need of reexamination.

In an appropriate case, I believe that we must further reconsider our "substantial effects" test with an eye toward constructing a standard that reflects the text and history of the Commerce Clause without totally rejecting our more recent Commerce Clause jurisprudence.

Today, however, I merely support the Court's conclusion with a discussion of the text, structure, and history of the Commerce Clause and an analysis of our early case law. My goal is simply to show how far we have departed from the original understanding and to demonstrate that the result we reach today is by no means "radical," see post, at ____ (STEVENS, J., dissenting). I also want to point out the necessity of refashioning a coherent test that does not tend to "obliterate the distinction between what is national and what is local and create a completely centralized government." Jones & Laughlin Steel Corp., supra, at 37, 57 S.Ct., at 624.

I

At the time the original Constitution was ratified, "commerce" consisted of selling, buying, and bartering, as well as transporting for these purposes. See 1 S. Johnson, A Dictionary of the English Language 361 (4th ed. 1773) (defining commerce as "Intercour[s]e; exchange of one thing for another; interchange of any thing; trade; traffick"); N. Bailey, An Universal Etymological English Dictionary (26th ed. 1789) ("trade or traffic"); T. Sheridan, A Complete Dictionary of the English Language (6th ed. 1796) ("Exchange of one thing for another; trade, traffick"). This understanding finds support in the etymology of the word, which literally means "with merchandise." See 3 Oxford English Dictionary 552 (2d ed. 1989) (com—"with"; merci—"merchandise"). In fact, when Federalists and Anti-Federalists discussed the Commerce Clause during the ratification period, they often used trade (in its selling/bartering sense) and commerce interchangeably. See The Federalist No. 4, p. 22 (J. Jay) (asserting that countries will cultivate our friendship when our "trade" is prudently regulated by Federal Government); 1 id., No. 7, at 39-40 (A. Hamilton) (discussing "competitions of commerce" between States resulting from state "regulations of trade"); id., No. 40, at 262 (J. Madison) (asserting that it was an "acknowledged object of the Convention . . . that the regulation of trade should be submitted to the general government"); Lee, Letters of a Federal Farmer No. 5, in Pamphlets on the Constitution of the United States 319 (P. Ford ed. 1888); Smith, An Address to the People of the State of New York, in id., at 107.

As one would expect, the term "commerce" was used in contradistinction to productive activities such as manufacturing and agriculture. Alexander Hamilton, for example, repeatedly treated commerce, agriculture, and manufacturing as three separate endeavors. See, e.g., The Federalist No. 36, at 224 (referring to "agriculture, commerce, manufactures"); id., No. 21, at 133 (distinguishing commerce, arts, and industry); id., No. 12, at 74 (asserting that commerce and agriculture have shared interests). The same distinctions were made in the state ratification conventions. See e.g., 2 Debates in the Several State Conventions on the Adoption of the Federal Constitution 57 (J. Elliot ed. 1836) (hereinafter Debates) (T. Dawes at Massachusetts convention); id., at 336 (M. Smith at New York convention).

Moreover, interjecting a modern sense of commerce into the Constitution generates significant textual and structural problems. For example, one cannot replace "commerce" with a different type of enterprise, such as manufacturing. When a manufacturer produces a car, assembly cannot take place "with a foreign nation" or "with the Indian Tribes." Parts may come from different States or other nations and hence may have been in the flow of commerce at one time, but manufacturing takes place at a discrete site. Agriculture and manufacturing involve the production of goods; commerce encompasses traffic in such articles.

The Port Preference Clause also suggests that the term "commerce" denoted sale and/or transport rather than business generally. According to that Clause, "[n]o Preference shall be given by any Regulation of Commerce or Revenue to the Ports of one State over those of another." U.S. Const., Art. I, § 9, cl. 6. Although it is possible to conceive of regulations of manufacturing or farming that prefer one port over another, the more natural reading is that the Clause prohibits Congress from using its commerce power to channel commerce through certain favored ports.

The Constitution not only uses the word "commerce" in a narrower sense than our case law might suggest, it also does not support the proposition that Congress has authority over all activities that "substantially affect" interstate commerce. The Commerce Clause 2 does not state that Congress may "regulate matters that substantially affect commerce with foreign Nations, and among the several States, and with the Indian Tribes." In contrast, the Constitution itself temporarily prohibited amendments that would "affect" Congress' lack of authority to prohibit or restrict the slave trade or to enact unproportioned direct taxation. U.S. Const., Art. V. Clearly, the Framers could have drafted a Constitution that contained a "substantially affects interstate commerce" clause had that been their objective.

In addition to its powers under the Commerce Clause, Congress has the authority to enact such laws as are "necessary and proper" to carry into execution its power to regulate commerce among the several States. U.S. Const., Art. I, § 8, cl. 18. But on this Court's understanding of congressional power under these two Clauses, many of Congress' other enumerated powers under Art. I, § 8 are wholly superfluous. After all, if Congress may regulate all matters that substantially affect commerce, there is no need for the Constitution to specify that Congress may enact bankruptcy laws, cl. 4, or coin money and fix the standard of weights and measures, cl. 5, or punish counterfeiters of United States coin and securities, cl. 6. Likewise, Congress would not need the separate authority to establish post offices and post roads, cl. 7, or to grant patents and copyrights, cl. 8, or to "punish Piracies and Felonies committed on the high Seas," cl. 10. It might not even need the power to raise and support an Army and Navy, cls. 12 and 13, for fewer people would engage in commercial shipping if they thought that a foreign power could expropriate their property with ease. Indeed, if Congress could regulate matters that substantially affect interstate commerce, there would have been no need to specify that Congress can regulate international trade and commerce with the Indians. As the Framers surely understood, these other branches of trade substantially affect interstate commerce.

Put simply, much if not all of Art. I, § 8 (including portions of the Commerce Clause itself) would be surplusage if Congress had been given authority over matters that substantially affect interstate commerce. An interpretation of cl. 3 that makes the rest of § 8 superfluous simply cannot be correct. Yet this Court's Commerce Clause jurisprudence has endorsed just such an interpretation: the power we have accorded Congress has swallowed Art. I, § 8.3

Indeed, if a "substantial effects" test can be appended to the Commerce Clause, why not to every other power of the Federal Government? There is no reason for singling out the Commerce Clause for special treatment. Accordingly, Congress could regulate all matters that "substantially affect" the Army and Navy, bankruptcies, tax collection, expenditures, and so on. In that case, the clauses of § 8 all mutually overlap, something we can assume the Founding Fathers never intended.

Our construction of the scope of congressional authority has the additional problem of coming close to turning the Tenth Amendment on its head. Our case law could be read to reserve to the United States all powers not expressly prohibited by the Constitution. Taken together, these fundamental textual problems should, at the very least, convince us that the "substantial effects" test should be reexamined.

II

BAN ASSAULT BANANAS

The exchanges during the ratification campaign reveal the relatively limited reach of the Commerce Clause and of federal power generally. The Founding Fathers confirmed that most areas of life (even many matters that would have substantial effects on commerce) would remain outside the reach of the Federal Government. Such affairs would continue to be under the exclusive control of the States.

Early Americans understood that commerce, manufacturing, and agriculture, while distinct activities, were intimately related and dependent on each other—that each "substantially affected" the others. After all, items produced by farmers and manufacturers were the primary articles of commerce at the time. If commerce was more robust as a result of federal superintendence, farmers and manufacturers could benefit. Thus, Oliver Ellsworth of Connecticut attempted to convince farmers of the benefits of regulating commerce. "Your property and riches depend on a ready demand and generous price for the produce you can annually spare," he wrote, and these conditions exist "where trade flourishes and when the merchant can freely export the produce of the country" to nations that will pay the highest price. A Landholder No. 1, Connecticut Courant, Nov. 5, 1787, in 3 Documentary History of the Ratification of the Constitution 399 (M. Jensen ed. 1978) (hereinafter Documentary History). See also The Federalist No. 35, at 219 (A. Hamilton) ("[D]iscerning citizens are well aware that the mechanic and manufacturing arts furnish the materials of mercantile enterprise and industry. Many of them indeed are immediately connected with the operations of commerce. They know that the merchant is their natural patron and friend"); id., at 221 ("Will not the merchant . . . be disposed to cultivate . . . the interests of the mechanic and manufacturing arts to which his commerce is so nearly allied?"); A Jerseyman: To the Citizens of New Jersey, Trenton Mercury, Nov. 6, 1787, in 3 Documentary History 147 (noting that agriculture will serve as a "source of commerce"); Marcus, The New Jersey Journal, Nov. 14, 1787, id., at 152 (both the mechanic and the farmer benefit from the prosperity of commerce). William Davie, a delegate to the North Carolina Convention, illustrated the close link best: "Commerce, sir, is the nurse of [agriculture and manufacturing]. The merchant furnishes the planter with such articles as he cannot manufacture himself, and finds him a market for his produce. Agriculture cannot flourish if commerce languishes; they are mutually dependent on each other." 4 Debates 20.

Yet, despite being well aware that agriculture, manufacturing, and other matters substantially affected commerce, the founding generation did not cede authority over all these activities to Congress. Hamilton, for instance, acknowledged that the Federal Government could not regulate agriculture and like concerns:

"The administration of private justice between the citizens of the same State, the supervision of agriculture and of other concerns of a similar nature, all those things in short which are proper to be provided for by local legislation, can never be desirable cares of a general jurisdiction." The Federalist No. 17, at 106.

BAN ASSAULT BANANAS

In the unlikely event that the Federal Government would attempt to exercise authority over such matters, its effort "would be as troublesome as it would be nugatory." Ibid.4

The comments of Hamilton and others about federal power reflected the well-known truth that the new Government would have only the limited and enumerated powers found in the Constitution. See, e.g., 2 Debates 267-268 (A. Hamilton at New York convention) (noting that there would be just cause for rejecting the Constitution if it would enable the Federal Government to "alter, or abrogate . . . [a state's] civil and criminal institutions [or] penetrate the recesses of domestic life, and control, in all respects, the private conduct of individuals"); The Federalist No. 45, at 313 (J. Madison); 3 Debates 259 (J. Madison) (Virginia convention); R. Sherman & O. Ellsworth, Letter to Governor Huntington, Sept. 26, 1787, in 3 Documentary History 352; J. Wilson, Speech in the State House Yard, Oct. 6, 1787, in 2 id., at 167-168. Agriculture and manufacture, since they were not surrendered to the Federal Government, were state concerns. See The Federalist No. 34, at 212-213 (A. Hamilton) (observing that the "internal encouragement of agriculture and manufactures" was an object of state expenditure). Even before the passage of the Tenth Amendment, it was apparent that Congress would possess only those powers "herein granted" by the rest of the Constitution. U.S. Const., Art. I, § 1.

Where the Constitution was meant to grant federal authority over an activity substantially affecting interstate commerce, the Constitution contains an enumerated power over that particular activity. Indeed, the Framers knew that many of the other enumerated powers in § 8 dealt with matters that substantially affected interstate commerce. Madison, for instance, spoke of the bankruptcy power as being "intimately connected with the regulation of commerce." The Federalist No. 42, at 287. Likewise, Hamilton urged that "[i]f we mean to be a commercial people or even to be secure on our Atlantic side, we must endeavour as soon as possible to have a navy." Id., No. 24, at 157 (A. Hamilton).

In short, the Founding Fathers were well aware of what the principal dissent calls " 'economic . . . realities.' " See post, at ____ (BREYER, J.) (citing North American Co. v. SEC, 327 U.S. 686, 705, 66 S.Ct. 785, 796, 90 L.Ed. 945 (1946)). Even though the boundary between commerce and other matters may ignore "economic reality" and thus seem arbitrary or artificial to some, we must nevertheless respect a constitutional line that does not grant Congress power over all that substantially affects interstate commerce.

III

If the principal dissent's understanding of our early case law were correct, there might be some reason to doubt this view of the original understanding of the Constitution. According to that dissent, Chief Justice Marshall's opinion in Gibbons v. Ogden, 9 Wheat. 1, 6 L.Ed. 23 (1824) established that Congress may control all local activities that "significantly affect interstate commerce," post, at ____. And, "with the exception of one wrong turn subsequently corrected," this has been the "traditiona[l]" method of interpreting the Commerce Clause. Post, at ____ (citing Gibbons and United States v. Darby, 312 U.S. 100, 116-117, 61 S.Ct. 451, 458-459, 85 L.Ed. 609 (1941)).

In my view, the dissent is wrong about the holding and reasoning of Gibbons. Because this error leads the dissent to characterize the first 150 years of this Court's case law as a "wrong turn," I feel compelled to put the last 50 years in proper perspective.

A.

In Gibbons, the Court examined whether a federal law that licensed ships to engage in the "coasting trade" preempted a New York law granting a 30-year monopoly to Robert Livingston and Robert Fulton to navigate the State's waterways by steamship. In concluding that it did, the Court noted that Congress could regulate "navigation" because "[a]ll America . . . has uniformly understood, the word 'commerce,' to comprehend navigation. It was so unde rstood, and must have been so understood, when the constitution was framed." 9 Wheat., at 190. The Court also observed that federal power over commerce "among the several States" meant that Congress could regulate commerce conducted partly within a State. Because a portion of interstate commerce and foreign commerce would almost always take place within one or more States, federal power over interstate and foreign commerce necessarily would extend into the States. Id., at 194-196.

At the same time, the Court took great pains to make clear that Congress could not regulate commerce "which is completely internal, which is carried on between man and man in a State, or between different parts of the same State, and which does not extend to or affect other States." Id., at 194. Moreover, while suggesting that the Constitution might not permit States to regulate interstate or foreign commerce, the Court observed that "[i]nspection laws, quarantine laws, health laws of every description, as well as laws for regulating the internal commerce of a State" were but a small part "of that immense mass of legislation . . . not surrendered to a general government." Id., at 203. From an early moment, the Court rejected the notion that Congress can regulate everything that affects interstate commerce. That the internal commerce of the States and the numerous state inspection, quarantine, and health laws had substantial effects on interstate commerce cannot be doubted. Nevertheless, they were not "surrendered to the general government."

Of course, the principal dissent is not the first to misconstrue Gibbons. For instance, the Court has stated that Gibbons "described the federal commerce power with a breadth never yet exceeded." Wickard v. Filburn, 317 U.S. 111, 120, 63 S.Ct. 82, 87, 87 L.Ed. 122 (1942). See also Perez v. United States, 402 U.S. 146, 151, 91 S.Ct. 1357, 1360, 28 L.Ed.2d 686 (1971) (claiming that with Darby and Wickard, "the broader view of the Commerce Clause announced by Chief Justice Marshall had been restored"). I believe that this misreading stems from two statements in Gibbons.

First, the Court made the uncontroversial claim that federal power does not encompass "commerce " that "does not extend to or affect other States." 9 Wheat., at 194 (emphasis added). From this statement, the principal dissent infers that whenever an activity affects interstate commerce, it necessarily follows that Congress can regulate such activities. Of course, Chief Justice Marshall said no such thing and the inference the dissent makes cannot be drawn.

There is a much better interpretation of the "affect[s]" language: because the Court had earlier noted that the commerce power did not extend to wholly intrastate commerce, the Court was acknowledging that although the line between intrastate and interstate/foreign commerce would be difficult to draw, federal authority could not be construed to cover purely intrastate commerce. Commerce that did not affect another State could never be said to be commerce "among the several States."

But even if one were to adopt the dissent's reading, the "affect[s]" language, at most, permits Congress to regulate only intrastate commerce that substantially affects interstate and foreign commerce. There is no reason to believe that Chief Justice Marshall was asserting that Congress could regulate all activities that affect interstate commerce. See Ibid.

The second source of confusion stems from the Court's praise for the Constitution's division of power between the States and the Federal Government:

"The genius and character of the whole government seem to be, that its action is to be applied to all the external concerns of the nation, and to those internal concerns which affect the States generally; but not to those which are completely within a particular State, which do not affect other States, and with which it is not necessary to interfere, for the purpose of executing some of the general powers of the government." Id., at 195.

In this passage, the Court merely was making the well understood point that the Constitution commits matters of "national" concern to Congress and leaves "local" matters to the States. The Court was not saying that whatever Congress believes is a national matter becomes an object of federal control. The matters of national concern are enumerated in the Constitution: war, taxes, patents, and copyrights, uniform rules of naturalization and bankruptcy, types of commerce, and so on. See generally U.S. Const., Art. I, § 8. Gibbons' emphatic statements that Congress could not regulate many matters that affect commerce confirm that the Court did not read the Commerce Clause as granting Congress control over matters that "affect the States generally." 5 Gibbons simply cannot be construed as the principal dissent would have it.

B
I am aware of no cases prior to the New Deal that characterized the power flowing from the Commerce Clause as sweepingly as does our substantial effects test. My review of the case law indicates that the substantial effects test is but an innovation of the 20th century.

Even before Gibbons, Chief Justice Marshall, writing for the Court in Cohens v. Virginia, 6 Wheat. 264, 5 L.Ed. 257 (1821), noted that Congress had "no general right to punish murder committed within any of the States," id., at 426, and that it was "clear that congress cannot punish felonies generally," id., at 428. The Court's only qualification was that Congress could enact such laws for places where it enjoyed plenary powers—for instance, over the District of Columbia. Id., at 426. Thus, whatever effect ordinary murders, or robbery, or gun possession might have on interstate commerce (or on any other subject of federal concern) was irrelevant to the question of congressional power.6

United States v. Dewitt, 9 Wall. 41, 19 L.Ed. 593 (1870), marked the first time the Court struck down a federal law as exceeding the power conveyed by the Commerce Clause. In a two-page opinion, the Court invalidated a nationwide law prohibiting all sales of naphtha and illuminating oils. In so doing, the Court remarked that the Commerce Clause "has always been understood as limited by its terms; and as a virtual denial of any power to interfere with the internal trade and business of the separate States." Id., at 44. The law in question was "plainly a regulation of police," which could have constitutional application only where Congress had exclusive authority, such as the territories. Id., at 44-45. See also License Tax Cases, 5 Wall. 462, 470-471, 18 L.Ed. 497 (1867) (Congress cannot interfere with the internal commerce and business of a State); Trade-Mark Cases, 100 U.S. 82, 25 L.Ed. 550 (1879) (Congress cannot regulate internal commerce and thus may not establish national trademark registration).

In United States v. E.C. Knight Co., 156 U.S. 1, 15 S.Ct. 249, 39 L.Ed. 325 (1895), this Court held that mere attempts to monopolize the manufacture of sugar could not be regulated pursuant to the Commerce Clause. Raising echoes of the discussions of the Framers regarding the intimate relationship between commerce and manufacturing, the Court declared that "[c]ommerce succeeds to manufacture, and is not a part of it." Id., at 12, 15 S.Ct., at 253. The Court also approvingly quoted from Kidd v. Pearson, 128 U.S. 1, 20, 9 S.Ct. 6, 9-10, 32 L.Ed. 346 (1888):

" 'No distinction is more popular to the common mind, or more clearly expressed in economic and political literature, than that between manufacture and commerce. . . . . If it be held that the term [commerce] includes the regulation of all such manufactures as are intended to be the subject of commercial transactions in the future, it is impossible to deny that it would also include all productive industries that contemplate the same thing. The result would be that Congress would be invested . . . with the power to regulate, not only manufactures, but also agriculture, horticulture, stock raising, domestic fisheries, mining—in short, every branch of human industry.' " E.C. Knight, 156 U.S., at 14, 15 S.Ct., at 254.

If federal power extended to these types of production "comparatively little of business operations and affairs would be left for state control." Id., at 16, 15 S.Ct., at 255.

See also Newberry v. United States, 256 U.S. 232, 257, 41 S.Ct. 469, 474, 65 L.Ed. 913 (1921) ("It is settled . . . that the power to regulate interstate and foreign commerce does not reach whatever is essential thereto. Without agriculture, manufacturing, mining, etc., commerce could not exist, but this fact does not suffice to subject them to the control of Congress"). Whether or not manufacturing, agriculture, or other matters substantially affected interstate commerce was irrelevant.

As recently as 1936, the Court continued to insist that the Commerce Clause did not reach the wholly internal business of the States. See Carter v. Carter Coal Co., 298 U.S. 238, 308, 56 S.Ct. 855, 871-872, 80 L.Ed. 1160 (1936) (Congress may not regulate mine labor because "[t]he relation of employer and employee is a local relation"); see also A.L.A. Schechter Poultry Corp. v. United States, 295 U.S. 495, 543-550, 55 S.Ct. 837, 848-852, 79 L.Ed. 1570 (1935) (holding that Congress may not regulate intrastate sales of sick chickens or the labor of employees involved in intrastate poultry sales). The Federal Government simply could not reach such subjects regardless of their effects on interstate commerce.

These cases all establish a simple point: from the time of the ratification of the Constitution to the mid-1930's, it was widely understood that the Constitution granted Congress only limited powers, notwithstanding the Commerce Clause.7 Moreover, there was no question that activities wholly separated from business, such as gun possession, were beyond the reach of the commerce power. If anything, the "wrong turn" was the Court's dramatic departure in the 1930's from a century and a half of precedent.

IV

Apart from its recent vintage and its corresponding lack of any grounding in the original understanding of the Constitution, the substantial effects test suffers from the further flaw that it appears to grant Congress a police power over the Nation. When asked at oral argument if there were any limits to the Commerce Clause, the Government was at a loss for words. Tr. of Oral Arg. 5. Likewise, the principal dissent insists that there are limits, but it cannot muster even one example. Post, at ___. Indeed, the dissent implicitly concedes that its reading has no limits when it criticizes the Court for "threaten[ing] legal uncertainty in an area of law that . . . seemed reasonably well settled." Post, at ____-____. The one advantage of the dissent's standard is certainty: it is certain that under its analysis everything may be regulated under the guise of the Commerce Clause.

The substantial effects test suffers from this flaw, in part, because of its "aggregation principle." Under so-called "class of activities" statutes, Congress can regulate whole categories of activities that are not themselves either "interstate" or "commerce." In applying the effects test, we ask whether the class of activities as a whole substantially affects interstate commerce, not whether any specific activity within the class has such effects when considered in isolation. See Maryland v. Wirtz, 392 U.S., at 192-193, 88

S.Ct., at 2021-2022 (if class of activities is " 'within the reach of federal power,' " courts may not excise individual applications as trivial) (quoting Darby, 312 U.S., at 120-121, 61 S.Ct., at 460-461).

The aggregation principle is clever, but has no stopping point. Suppose all would agree that gun possession within 1,000 feet of a school does not substantially affect commerce, but that possession of weapons generally (knives, brass knuckles, nunchakus, etc.) does. Under our substantial effects doctrine, even though Congress cannot single out gun possession, it can prohibit weapon possession generally. But one always can draw the circle broadly enough to cover an activity that, when taken in isolation, would not have substantial effects on commerce. Under our jurisprudence, if Congress passed an omnibus "substantially affects interstate commerce" statute, purporting to regulate every aspect of human existence, the Act apparently would be constitutional. Even though particular sections may govern only trivial activities, the statute in the aggregate regulates matters that substantially affect commerce.

V

This extended discussion of the original understanding and our first century and a half of case law does not necessarily require a wholesale abandonment of our more recent opinions.8 It simply reveals that our substantial effects test is far removed from both the Constitution and from our early case law and that the Court's opinion should not be viewed as "radical" or another "wrong turn" that must be corrected in the future.9 The analysis also suggests that we ought to temper our Commerce Clause jurisprudence.

Unless the dissenting Justices are willing to repudiate our long-held understanding of the limited nature of federal power, I would think that they too must be willing to reconsider the substantial effects test in a future case. If we wish to be true to a Constitution that does not cede a police power to the Federal Government, our Commerce Clause's boundaries simply cannot be "defined" as being " 'commensurate with the national needs' " or self-consciously intended to let the Federal Government " 'defend itself against economic forces that Congress decrees inimical or destructive of the national economy.' " See post, at ____-____ (BREYER, J., dissenting) (quoting North American Co. v. SEC, 327 U.S. 686, 705, 66 S.Ct. 785, 796, 90 L.Ed. 945 (1946)). Such a formulation of federal power is no test at all: it is a blank check.

At an appropriate juncture, I think we must modify our Commerce Clause jurisprudence. Today, it is easy enough to say that the Clause certainly does not empower Congress to ban gun possession within 1,000 feet of a school.

www.ingramcontent.com/pod-product-compliance
Lightning Source LLC
Chambersburg PA
CBHW052312220526
45472CB00001B/80